A SONG FOR KALEN

LESSONS FROM THE LIFE AND DEATH OF MY SON

T.R. SHERLOCK

ISBN: 978-1-953610-50-8

    1. Memoir
    2. Autobiography
    3. Social Issue> Families in Crisis
    4. Social Issues> Violence in Society
    5. Family Loss> Coping

NFB
<<<>>>
NFB Publishing/Amelia Press
119 Dorchester Road
Buffalo, New York 14213

For more information visit
Nfbpublishing.com

PREFACE

During our time on earth, if we keep our eyes and hearts open, we will experience incredible gifts. The red and golden leaves on a full tree flickering gently in the wind. A comforting hug from a loved one. The ability to express our creativity. I believe these experiences, these moments, are indeed gifts.

Some people call them miracles. By definition, a miracle is an extraordinary experience where the divine intervenes in human affairs. Do miracles even exist? How often do people call out in despair for divine intervention, but the world keeps turning? How many times have humans prayed and pleaded for a miracle that never came? However, there are rare moments, when we experience something so surreal, we have no answer as to why it happened. These events that transcend all understanding - these are our miracles.

Life is finite. It is limited. We live and we die, and the latter happens in many forms and fashions. For me, God delivered a gift so profound it changed my life forever. That gift, that miracle, was my children. As a father, I traversed the bookends of life. I have felt pure elation that could reach the heavens. I have also felt the kind of pain words can never describe – not even all the words in this book. Through every chapter of life and every experience, we face lessons and choices we must make. We discover our strength as human beings. We feel and we grow. We experience joy, love, betrayal, anger, and yes, forgiveness.

The greatest miracle is survival. It is rising from the smoldering ashes of the fires that destroy and consume us, to soar. It is to change and transcend tragedy, to discover the light that remains. Only the greatest of tragedies can create this miracle. Through the death of my son Kalen, I have recognized many gifts. This is his story – our story – of birth, death, and living. It is a story of hope, strength, and forgiveness; of lessons and perseverance. These are Kalen's lyrics, penned not just as the result of the miracle he bestowed upon us in our deepest despair, but as a gift to those who hear his song.

ACKNOWLEGEMENTS

THE CREATION OF THIS book began as nothing more than a conversation when Pamela Say reached out, asking if she could feature my story in her publication. I felt honored to be featured by a global news organization, and to have that article written by my friend. Little did I know where it would lead. *A Song for Kalen* has become a book of redemption, hope, forgiveness, and healing for me. I want to fist thank Pam for her countless hours of editing, the long phone calls to help me find my words and voice, and the time spent crying with me when I felt I could not breath from the grief that spilled onto the page.

Secondly, I want to thank my family and especially my son Karter, for always inspiring me to reach for the stars and constantly reminding me that hard work and dedication pay off. I want to thank him for allowing me to be his dad and to make mistakes.

Special recognition must also go to my family for allowing me to relive each detail over again, to make sure that this story honored the memory of Kalen fully. To The Sharing Hope Foundation, thank you for all the love and support throughout the journey of making Kalen an organ doner. To the staff at McLeod Hospital, thank you for your care and dedication during my son's hospitalization, and especially to Nurse Rachel for the strength, understanding, caring, and love in the gifts you gave me and in your presence in my darkest hour.

Lastly to my son, my angel, my Kalen: thank you for the gift of being your dad; for the peace and the lessons you bestowed upon me during your short time on Earth through your spirit, love, humor, and sense of wonder. The lessons contained in this book are the lessons Kalen taught me through his birth, life, and death - lessons I now pass on to you, the reader.

TABLE OF CONTENTS

ONE:
GAY MEN CAN'T BE DADS

CHILDREN SO OFTEN DREAM of the things they want to be when they grow up – a pilot, a rock star, a scientist, a dancer. My entire life, I just wanted to be a father. At five years old as a little boy running around the backyard playing kids' games, I knew one thing clearly. Being a dad seemed like the coolest job ever.

I centered my whole life around being a father. Having a profession came secondary to that. It did not matter what else I did in my life if I was a parent first. That desire shaped many of my ideas and beliefs growing up, both good and bad.

I was raised in a traditional Roman Catholic home. I am also a gay man. The convergence between my upbringing and what I understood to be acceptable in society clashed with an identity I had not yet fully formulated. How was I going to be a dad? How could someone like me raise a child? My answer came early. I could never come out, nor did I fully understand at that young age what coming out even meant. I just knew something had to be suppressed.

As early as eleven or twelve, I remember going through that confusing and awkward stage when hormones kick in and social flirtation begins. Attractions are not yet sexual, at least they weren't for me. I was drawn to both boys and girls. Yet, I knew what I had seen and been told. Boys date girls. So, that is what I did.

In middle school, my version of dating was to hold hands with a girl and watch television together. It felt very innocent until high school, when I became involved with a musical at the local theatre. I met a gentleman there and immediately became smitten by him. I had my first sexual experience and I felt whole and complete. It was like, for the first time in my life, I knew who I was. Soon after, I sat down with my mother at the kitchen table and explained what happened. I told her I was gay or, if nothing else, I was bisexual. My mom warned me to be careful putting that label on in the world. She said once you do, you cannot take it back. There is a great stigma that goes along with it. She suggested I make sure this was who I was, and not just a phase.

My beautiful mother, who I loved and respected, gave me a warning. The world can be a very judgmental place. She wasn't mean about it, and she meant no harm. Rather, she wanted to protect me. Something happened inside of me at that moment. A piece of me shut down. This feeling of wholeness – this deep, gut-level truth in my soul, I had just discovered – was not in the cards. I was not allowed to be gay.

That proved a pivotal moment for me. The two things I knew most about myself – that I liked men and that I wanted to be a dad – could not exist simultaneously in this one life. So, if nothing else, I grasped tightly to my dream to be a father. I would never let go of my deep desire to be a dad.

In high school I met a gorgeous girl who, as a teenager, had a child. I felt I found my opportunity to be a surrogate dad to a beautiful little boy and find out if being with a woman elicited the same response as my earlier encounter with a man. The sex felt wonderful and suddenly, I thought the world made sense again; I could be with a woman. This solved all my problems.

After my high school girlfriend and I broke up, and I would soon be off to college, the world became my oyster. My dream to find a partner – a wife – and have a family could happen someday so I let myself enjoy being a student. I lived in the dorms, studied, and went to college parties, but remained ever the romantic. I would find real love.

In my first college romance, she and I decided to pace ourselves. We stayed friends throughout our freshman year and started dating in our sophomore year. I wanted to marry her! The entire novel played out in my head: we would finish college, have a beautiful wedding, start making babies, and live happily ever after in our perfect home. Our junior year seemed a better time than ever to begin practicing for all the joy yet to come, so I quit my job as a resident assistant, and we moved into an apartment off campus. It felt like everything in life began to fall into place, then another piece of news came. She was pregnant. It seemed far too soon and not in our plans, but the dreams I had from a young age leapt back into my mind. I felt ecstatic. She did not feel the same way; rather, she felt adamant, she could not keep the baby.

While this pregnancy represented the culmination of all my hopes and dreams, I knew she had the right to choose for her own body. My heart broke, but I pushed it aside and vowed to be noble; to be a man of my word. Unable to put the procedure on her insurance, I borrowed $200 from my mother and added $200 of my own money, and we went to the clinic.

At that time, early in a pregnancy, a woman could take one pill by mouth and insert several others vaginally to induce the miscarriage. She could not bring herself to do it on her own. It was too hard, so I did it for her. As we went through the steps, the emotional pain tore me apart inside. I had to confront the devastating truth of what I was doing to my own child. I believed in the right to choose, and I still do; but I also experienced how hard that choice is to make.

Soon after, my girlfriend left me. Too much pain existed between us, and she struggled to see me as she had before. My heart ached from the loss, and I decided to take a semester and a half off college before going back for my junior year. By then, I felt so much older. Graduation loomed in front of me, and adult questions bounced around my mind. What classes should I take? What is my career going to be? If I want to get married one day, I better start looking! I may have only been in my mid-twenties, but my biological clock sounded like a train whistle in my head.

One of my friends – always on the lookout – told me one night that she had the perfect person for me. She introduced me to yet another woman. Little did I know this young woman standing before me would become my wife and mother to my two beautiful boys.

Two:
Love at First Sight

My new female friend worked in the daycare on campus and studied special education, while I pursued a double major in English and psychology. Right away we had a lot in common. She had good grades, life goals, and thought about her career. We enjoyed a long and traditional courting period before we ever became intimately involved, and I really respected her for that. She graduated and moved back to her hometown, while I stayed behind in Fredonia to finish up as a super senior year with a double major and a double minor. Our relationship never wavered.

After Commencement, I moved to Clyde, NY and she and I got engaged. We had been together for a year already and waited another year to tie the knot. As soon as we said our vows, we started trying for kids. For another year, the little line on the pregnancy test that came so quickly and unexpectedly for my last girlfriend, alluded us time and again. The first few months, it felt like a normal part of the process. "Don't worry," I would tell her, "It will happen," but after five months my own fear kicked in.

What if I can't have kids, after all of this? What if there is something wrong with my sperm or with her eggs? What if the birth control affected her? We began to panic and realized it was time to go see a doctor. He assured us there was nothing wrong, so round two of trying to have babies began! We planned sex around her ovulation, but every negative result left us more and more defeated. She felt devastated so I took on the role of supportive husband, while I grappled with my own fears. A thought came to my mind. If we can't have kids, did I do all of this for nothing? What will happen to my dream of becoming a father?

Distraught, I sought support at home and my mother told me to forget about it; stop trying. She said I was putting too much pressure on myself, and the stress was not helping. So, we let go of all attempts to have a baby and – BAM – we got pregnant.

Imagine for a moment, a little girl who dreamed of being a pilot her entire life. She zoomed around the backyard with little airplanes. She looked longingly at pictures of Amelia Earhart. She tipped her head back on a bright summer day and stared up into the sky as jets flew by. The years passed and she worked extra hard to qualify for an academy and the day she stepped onto her first airplane as a student, the goosebumps became visible on her skin. She wasn't just walking into a cockpit like a kid on a fieldtrip. Her dreams were coming true as the plane flashed through the wild blue!

That was what becoming a father was like for me. I could not wait to do all the silly things new parents do. We bought onesies that said grandma and grandpa, and nana and papa. We invited our parents over for dinner and gave them our announcement gifts as we beamed with anticipation. They were ecstatic! This was a dream come true for everyone.

Our first pregnancy went splendidly, right up until the delivery. As we sat at home, suddenly it appeared that her water broke, and we rushed to the hospital. The doctors informed us she had a high leak, and the baby's position acted as a plug, stopping the fluid from coming out. Our regular doctor went out of town, so they advised us to wait at home, with her on bed rest for mild cramping. "If the apple is ripe, it will fall from the tree," they said. During the weekend our doctor arrived and informed us we could not wait, and insisted she be induced that Tuesday.

What a magical day for me! We got up bright and early and readied the bag we packed the night before. We took pictures and her parents came out for the photos. It was B-day – the birth of our first-born son! My heart soared with excitement.

At the hospital, a normal labor ensued. She went through the typical contractions and finally at 11:30 a.m. they broke her water. We opted for a natural birth because she didn't want any medication, but a half hour into labor, she shouted, "I want drugs! Give me the epidural!"

The anesthesiologist came in to give her the shot but as soon as they sat her up in bed, she jerked in pain. The anesthesiologist said, honey, you can't move while I administer the epidural. My wife responded, "You can't do this right now. He is coming." They insisted she was just feeling pressure and she shouted, "No! I am not." The anesthesiologist looked down and confirmed, "She's crowning!" The nurses rolled her down the hallway and paged the doctor who was at his office across the street. I watched out the window as he ran towards the hospital building, his tie flying sideways alongside him. He didn't even have time to put scrubs on. He simply demanded a pair of gloves.

With the situation clearly urgent he told my wife, "I want you to give me one good push," and she did. That was all it took! Karter shot out like a force to be reckoned with as if he were making a grand entrance: "Hello world! Here I am." It was amazing.

They placed our perfect little son on my wife's chest while he cried out his very first sounds and I cut the cord. I looked up from him and that is when I realized my wife was not moving. A flurry ensued. The voices rang out in urgent, short sentences:

"She passed out."

"She is hemorrhaging."

"We have to go NOW."

"She needs surgery."

The voices took over the room and in a moment of consciousness she asked, "Where's my baby?" I told her the baby was fine and she demanded, "Do not let anyone touch him," just as they rolled her away.

The surgery lasted three hours as they worked to repair a perpendicular, t-shaped tear in the birth canal. It took more stitches than could be counted to save her life. Throughout her surgery, I waited quietly in the hospital room with my son. I would not let anyone come in and see him. I wanted her to hold Karter before the world swarmed in around him.

In the quietness of the room, I gave him his first bath and swaddled him tightly in a blanket. I sat in the rocking chair the entire time, holding him, singing to him, and rocking him gently in my arms. He never cried. He just looked up at me cooing, that perfect baby scent rising off his skin. The tears streamed down my cheeks, and I knew, this was it. This is what I was always meant to do. As verbose as I can be, one word came to my mind repeatedly: Wow.

I became utterly speechless. Karter served as my first true understanding of life's greatest gifts. This little creature - this perfect human being with his long arms and gangly legs, his spindly fingers, his peach-fuzzy, brownish-blonde hair, and his beautiful little smile – he was mine and I was his. I leaned down to him and I whispered, "I'm your daddy. Out of all the daddies in the whole world you chose me."

That is how I always felt about my boys. These little spirits, these beings, were a gift to me. It was nothing to take on all the duties of fatherhood and, with my wife's surgery, she could not get up and move for some time. So, I went into daddy and mommy mode. I took paternity leave, changed diapers, made meals, got up in the middle of the night, cleaned, cooked, and even made homemade baby food.

Eventually as she recovered, she decided to go back to work, and I would stay home. For some time, it was me and Karter. I took him to the doctor and when he was sick, I got up with him. Dinner was ready every night and I served it at the table. Oh god, did I want more kids! There was no greater joy – no higher high – than being a father. Sadly, the roles we took on set off a dynamic that would lead to the demise of our marriage, and I quickly felt something was missing.

THREE:

HIS NAME IS KALEN

As TIME PASSED, MY marriage to my wife slowly fell apart. We talked about divorce, then news of a second pregnancy came. I stayed for six months hoping things might improve but it became abundantly clear to me, the situation could not be reconciled. All the things that happened in preparation for Karter's birth – the celebrating, packing of bags, and making grand announcements – stripped away the second time around. We separated.

One day, at the end of the pregnancy, she called and asked me to pick Karter up at daycare. She said she had a stress test appointment. I picked Karter up and took him to my apartment, where her parents would come and collect him at 5:30 p.m. The time came and went. It seemed very unlike my former in-laws. At 6:30 p.m. I picked up the phone and found out she was still at the doctor, so I went about my evening. I made Karter dinner, placed his pajamas out, and drew a bath. The minutes ticked by, and no one responded to my continued calls. My mind began swirling with questions, which escalated into concerns.

Finally, my worry intensified enough that I called the hospital looking for my soon to be ex-wife. The voice on the end of the line said, "We can't give out patient information." I replied, "She is my wife. I am her husband and the father of her baby." My heart stopped when the voice replied, "We have been directed not to provide you with any information."

I placed the phone down, stunned and in disbelief. Those feelings soon turned into a sense of betrayal and fury. How could a human being treat someone like this? I later found out her appointment was not for a stress test, but to induce and begin labor. She knew she was having the baby that day and deliberately withheld it from me. The thoughts battling in my head tossed me about emotionally; I felt overwhelmed with pain, doubt, and fear. What if something is wrong? Would she tell me? Is this a game?

I called the hospital again, and I contacted an attorney to learn about my rights. If I had to fight, I would fight – not with her or for myself, but for my kids. That is what it means to be a dad. As parents, it isn't about us or our issues; it's about them. This moment, though awful, became another gift in my life. It revealed the type of father I wanted to be - to never vilify her; to allow my children to grow up knowing love, kindness, compassion and understanding. Even as I sat there in that moment knowing my new baby was coming into the world – while my first son splashed around in the bathtub – I vowed to show them daddy is willing to work with mommy. But first, I had to fight.

By 7:30 the next morning, I retained an attorney, and my mom made the three-hour drive to be with me. We walked into the hospital side-by-side and an executive met us at the door. "I'm so sorry about this," the administrator said. "This is very unorthodox. The mother is adamant she doesn't want to see you. Is there any way we can do this during a different part of the day?" I replied with a crystal clear, "No," so he took us upstairs where we encountered her mother. Upon seeing me, she declared, "How dare you," as if my presence were an affront to everyone. "How dare me," I asked. "Your daughter deliberately played this out. That is my son, and I will see him. Get out of my way."

The hospital staff put me in my own room to fill out the paternity paperwork and to bond with my son. It was a typical hospital room with a neatly made bed flanked by a chair in the corner. The nurse wheeled in a plastic basinet that said "Sherlock" on the little card. My newborn son lay gently inside, wrapped up tight with a little blue hat on. I leaned down, unwrapped him, and changed his diaper. I outfitted him in a new onesie and gave him a hat with little duckies on it. I lifted him up and rocked him gently as I sang *My Funny Valentine*. My boy weighed six pounds and stretched 21.25 inches. He looked like a cherub with perfect, little fat rolls. I fell instantly in love. In that moment, nothing was wrong in the world. Karter climbed up on my lap and held Kalen with me.

Soon after, my wife asked to see both boys together. I insisted on being in the room, for fear she would try to take them away from me. Karter climbed up with his mother. I stood back silently as they took family photographs, before the hospital staff asked me to step into the hallway to fill out a few more papers. My mother-in-law followed me out and demanded, "I can't believe you are forcing her to do this. She doesn't want the baby to have your name." The law was on my side, so I signed the paperwork, including acknowledgment of paternity, and went back in the room. By then Kalen began fussing and needed to be fed so I excused myself and Karter, though they fought me and tried to keep Karter there. After that we only communicated regarding the children and the court proceedings.

Even as this dramatic and devastating scene played out before me, I remember thinking mostly about those two boys. "How can I love another child? Can I love them equally?" Yet, the minute I saw my second son, my Kalen, in that hospital room, my heart grew a size larger. I realized love did not have some imaginary limit to its capacity. The love for Kalen just seemed to always be there, as if my soul had expanded. I just loved more.

In the first months, I kept Karter while my wife stayed home with Kalen. When Kalen turned three months old, I won in court for overnight visits. Being with my sons became all that mattered. Kalen proved quite a baby! He never fussed, never became colicky, and always slept through the night. Even when he later developed issues with his ears, he remained happy-go-lucky. Kalen hardly ever cried but when he did cry, he really cried! Karter felt absolutely enamored with his brother. From the moment Kalen entered this world, Karter did everything for him; he wanted to be close to him all the time.

FOUR:
PART-TIME PARENT

WATCHING MY BOYS GROW up proved fascinating and beautiful. They quickly became each other's best friends, figuratively and literally. If they got in trouble, they did it together. Where you found one you found the other. Still, being a part-time dad took a toll on me. It did not match the dreams of fatherhood I had for all those years.

On the days I had my boys, we did everything; the house filled with laughter and noise. Yet, I became the every-other-weekend father. In the two weeks that followed a visit, the weight of the silence felt so heavy it crushed me. The disappearance of their laughter lingered in the air until the silence became deafening. I had no messes to pick up; no little voices asking for snacks. I went to visit family and friends to bide my time. When I saw other people with their kids, it only reminded me that mine were missing. I felt like a puzzle, absent the most important piece.

The constant court dates piled up on top of the loneliness I felt. The repeated sense of loss and purpose when my boys left devastated me. Every couple of months we went back to court. I constantly pled for more time and tried to address the issues I knew were going on back in their primary home. When I had my boys, I felt pure joy. When they left, a cavern grew inside of me so deep, it would soon spin me into addiction. When they left, I did not want to feel anything, but when I had them, I felt pure elation.

The long summer days became a favorite. We often went camping. Karter would go fishing while Kalen oooo'd and aaah'd in his pack and play. I taught them how to swim. When Kalen began talking, he could not say dad, so he called me Dee Dee. This would become my name from that point on. I remember him flexing his muscles to show everyone how big and strong he was. Right out of the gate, he seemed in a hurry to grow up.

Birthdays also felt like an especially amazing time. Since the boys were two years, five days, and six hours apart, I could celebrate my two greatest gifts together. On Kalen's first birthday and Karter's third, we had a big blowout Halloween-themed costume party. The kids flailed around in the giant bounce house we rented. I dressed Kalen as a little pumpkin with white walking shoes. He stumbled around – a cute, little jack-o-lantern with legs. He just wanted to run and crawl with all the other kids. When the time came to blow out the candle, he smooshed his whole face into a cupcake and let out a full belly laugh so infectious I felt it way down inside of me. I had my dream, right there, giggling in front of me. I sat there watching my two sons at the party thinking, this is what my life is supposed to be.

Another amazing time for us, like many families, was Christmas. I would make an amazing dinner and we would frost cookies and watch Polar Express. We reveled in the excitement of Christmas mornings. I never missed a date or visitation except twice in five years, once due to a blizzard and once due to a flood, each of which closed the roads. I attended every doctor's appointment I knew about. I felt being a father and doing everything I could for my sons remained a duty. When I looked at them, I knew I did not create these delightful little humans. They may be a part of me, but they were also gifts. I had a responsibility to instill all the good and right things into them.

I did everything in my power to be the best dad, but when the boys left, I fell completely apart. The drive from my home back to Seneca Falls felt like a prolonged death. When I dropped off the boys, I cried the entire way back home. The car seemed eerily quiet. Their presence brought me to a joyful climax and leaving them felt like actual torture. It plummeted me into the darkest of places. Every time they left, it felt like all I had was their memories to live on. My heart broke over and over and over again.

Soon, a pattern emerged. I would get home and drink or use drugs to oblivion. I would go to work, come home, and use until Friday when I had to pick them up. I would put it all away for their arrival and become a dad again. During those years, something went missing from my soul. The boys did not see my alcoholism, but when they went home, I transformed into a full-blown addict.

Everything slipped out of my hands, and I felt powerless to change it. I did not see my boys much at all. Weird thoughts entered my mind as a deep sense of loss permeated every cell in my body. On their third and fifth birthdays, I had photos taken of them in matching shirts. When the pictures came back, I remember thinking, what if one of them was ever missing from the picture? What if I never have a moment like this again? Perhaps it was a premonition of things to come.

Outside of my addiction, everything I ever did in life centered around my kids; but addiction became another part of me. When I used, I felt a profound bottom because I knew I failed my children. I did not feel shame for myself, my parents, or even over what the community thought of me. The greatest tragedy was that my kids were slipping away, and I could not protect them. I was a hot, fucking mess.

As hard as I tried in court to get to my boys, by then, the court only saw a drug-addicted loser. I failed time and again to bring my sons home with me. This became enough motivation to make a decision. I needed to get sober so nothing could stand in the way of me and my boys. By then, I became aware that my ex-wife was using too, but in front of the kids and in the home. They lived in an unsafe environment. Out of desperation, I began to battle my own demons.

FIVE:
HAPPY, JOYOUS, AND FREE

WHEN I BEGAN TO drink while my sons were away, I could not have predicted the path sprawled out in front of me. I did not understand I had a disease called addiction. Many people have a beer or a glass of wine at night either for fun or when they are struggling with something. It doesn't make them alcoholics or addicts. This delineation never occurred to me. Looking back, I can see how addiction reared its head in my teens and young adulthood. However, I always viewed those moments as the typical "rite of passage." Kids and college students party. It seemed normal.

After I lost my boys and began to drink and use, something changed. It kicked off a compulsion I could no longer control. My life spiraled quickly. I wasn't working and the courts suspended my driver's license due to non-payment of child support. My parents had to drive me a city away to see the boys. When I had them, I swore they would never witness my addiction, but the disease made itself a priority.

It wasn't long before I would get sick if I didn't use every few hours, so I'd take a little after they went to bed to make it through. That lasted about a year, then I got careless, and the kids noticed. My ex-wife suspected what I was doing and, rightfully so, worried about letting me take Karter and Kalen. After one visit with the boys, Karter went home and told mommy that daddy sleeps a lot and has this white stuff that makes him goofy. She was done and the courts demanded I comply with supervised visitations. Sadly, this would not be my rock bottom.

A flurry of rapid changes swept me up in its wake in 2013 and I finally felt the disease drowning me. I stopped working, stopped paying rent, got evicted, and moved in with my aunt. Within two weeks, she threw me out. I couch surfed through April and May and by the end of June slept regularly at a shelter. When I couldn't do that anymore, in July, I became officially homeless. On those warm summer nights, I slept underneath a bridge or in the park. I ate out of garbage cans and lied to everyone.

In the middle of that month, our city's big Italian festival rolled into town, and I could not wait. I stopped by my aunt's house to use the bathroom and stole some vodka and prescription pills out of her medicine cabinet. Never had I been so intoxicated and high in my life. By then, I had some information. I'd been to the drug court and in the rooms of recovery, but I could fake it enough to get by. When my aunt found me sleeping on her porch the next morning, she kicked me and told me to leave.

It was quiet that Sunday. I began to walk up over First Street hill toward Lincoln Park, when I passed an apartment and saw a woman from the recovery program out sunbathing. "Holy fuck, you look bad," she said. Something clicked inside me. "I just want to die," I told her. "I'm done. I can't do this anymore." She took me inside and handed me a coffee as I sobbed. "I need help," I told her. I was due to appear in drug court on Tuesday. "Stay here tonight," she said, "Tomorrow we'll go talk to the coordinator." Monday came and I tried to find every reason not to go talk to the woman from drug court, but my friend insisted. When we arrived at the office she said, "You tell her exactly what you told me or I'm telling her." Defeated, I looked up and said, "I need rehab." I continued, "I need a halfway house and I need to be court ordered." "See me at court tomorrow," she responded.

Throughout the day I started going through withdrawals, shaking, and vomiting. In the courtroom, the judge called my name. I told him everything, but I tempered it. "I need two weeks," I said. "I need to prepare some things before I go in. I need to tell my ex-wife and the kids." The judge looked at me and said something I did not expect. "Tim, I'm so proud of you that I have a gift for you." A gift, I thought. "Cuff him," the judge said. "You are going to jail. You are doing it my way."

The judge did exactly what he said he would do. He sent me to jail until a bed opened up in rehab, and my journey back to sobriety, to fatherhood, and to my beautiful boys began. I went to rehab. At that same time, my ex-wife defied the Supreme Court Order and moved to South Carolina with my sons. I saw the program through anyway. The truth was I had two options: die or get help, so rehab it was. I made my decision in a total moment of desperation and in a prayer to God. I would get better, I would get my life together, and I would get my kids back.

I entered rehab in September and spent 31 days feeling agitated, like my skin was crawling. I attended constant groups and counseling. I learned during that time that I suffered with many mental health issues, and I learned to deal with my depression. I grew healthier than I had ever been in my life, began learning who I was, and started to love myself. No matter how many hours I spent on self-growth, though, my children always remained in the back of my mind. I constantly wondered if they were okay.

I called every day and night, but my calls went unanswered. After my time in the rehab, I faced the second phase of my recovery and entered a halfway house. Learning to live in the world without drugs remained imperative to getting my life together. I continued to try and connect with my kids every day. I looked at their photos and that great chasm of despair grew inside of me. Only this time, I held on to the truth: I would have them back. This truth helped me fight my anguish.

Successfully completing rehab and my time spent in the halfway house allowed me to rediscover joy in life. I appreciated the little things like nature and laughter. As I became honest with myself, I finally came out as gay. By fully accepting myself, I knew the future life I would share with my children would not be some social construct. It would be exactly what it was supposed to be.

I finally heard from my kids on Karter's birthday in October. A thrill overcame me as I wished them both a happy birthday and told them I was getting better and would see them soon. Then, something happened which suddenly turned my world dark. Karter said they were on a great adventure in North Carolina. My ex-wife informed me they left and were not coming back.

I could not understand what I was hearing. The divorce decree did not permit her to leave the state with the boys or move away. At one time in my life, this news would have destroyed me and sent me spiraling back into addiction and alcoholism. This time, it only fueled my determination to fight for my sons. I filed petition after petition in the courts to have my boys returned to me. It felt eerily similar to those early days of their lives, in and out of court. My family hired a private investigator and found out my boys were living in South Carolina. Still, I believed the law would be on my side. After all, I was clean and sober, and this time it appeared that my ex-wife was using.

I stayed loyal to my intentions and finished rehab, treatment, the halfway house experience, and full emersion into Alcoholics Anonymous. I had my life back and a plan to get my boys. I found myself standing in front of a judge, clean and sober. I knew the ramifications of children living immersed in the throes of an adult's addictions and I worried for my sons' safety. In that Allegany County Court room, I looked at the judge, totally dependent on his characterization of me.

"I am clean and sober," I asserted. "And I'm telling you, she will directly or indirectly kill one of my children." The judge looked at me and said, "Aren't you over dramatic?" I responded, "Your honor, I am an addict. I have lived that life."

While I could not prove it, I knew what was happening around my boys. My ex had a college education – a master's degree. She was a revered educator in the community; but me – they knew my history because I never lied about anything. The court ignored my plea, so I did the only thing I could, I decided to move to South Carolina to be closer to my sons. This was the only way I was going to be able to protect them. I was clean and stable, so I packed all my belongings in boxes and began to make arrangements for my move.

SIX:
SHATTERED

I<small>T WAS A</small> F<small>RIDAY</small>; just a plain, old, ordinary Friday. There was nothing more remarkable about this day of the week than any other. To be more specific, it was September 15, 2017. I woke up abruptly from a sound sleep at 4:00 a.m. Something startled me as if there had been an earthquake, but I live in New York State. We don't have many earthquakes. Everything seemed to be in place, so I tumbled out of bed. I made my way to the tiny gally-style kitchen in my one-bedroom apartment to make myself a cup of the holy nectar, coffee.

Carefully stepping around the boxes that were, in my mind, skillfully placed and in varying stages of being packed and sealed for my upcoming "big move," I looked out my tiny kitchen window. The sun was just beginning to soften the darkness into light gray as mother earth began to awaken with me. I looked through the boxes haphazardly as I drank my coffee and knew this move was the right decision. I was preparing to move to South Carolina in the next couple of weeks to be with my boys, my miracles. I had been sober for almost two years, and I was ready to be the dad I was always meant to be. The decision to move made sense. So much had changed in my life in such a short span of time. I had become clean and sober, gained my own place to live, and my legal problems were but a memory. I announced with all the vibrato of an opera singer that I was gay. Yes, I had grown indeed. I had been tested and forged into a new being. Little did I know my test, my transformation, was only a beginning.

I made my way from the window to the bathroom to ready myself for this ordinary Friday. Every Friday night I performed in a drag show - one of my many newfound hobbies in my new life. Still feeling somehow unsettled from my abrupt awakening that morning, I contemplated staying home. But as they say, the show must go on. I quickly showered and packed up my supplies and costumes, pushing away that uneasy feeling that was hanging over me. As usual, a friend picked me up and drove me into town to my friend Jeanne's house, where we gathered and loaded up the vehicles before heading to the venue.

The crew was there and getting ready, laughing, and bopping around like a clip out of "Girls Just Wanna Have Fun." The show was in Jamestown, some distance away, and we usually left around 12:30. I was smoking a cigarette and socializing when my phone started ringing. My mother-in-law's name appeared on the screen. I had not spoken to this woman much at all since divorcing her daughter three years ago, so what could she want out of nowhere, unless it was an emergency, or they needed something. Unease sunk into my stomach.

"I have to take this," I said to the girls. "It's not going to be good." I answered the phone with as upbeat of a hello as I could muster and her voice spoke softly, "Hey Tim, I need to talk to you." I could already hear something was off in the tentative way she was speaking.

"Okay, what's going on; is everything okay," I asked just as tentatively, feeling deep within me that I truly did not want her to answer that question.

What came next, no one can ever prepare for, or even imagine. What came next is the very thing that every parent has nightmares over, but always believes that it happens to other people, never to them. What came next washed over me like battery acid. In a truly clear and at the same time hurried voice, she told me there had been an accident, but that Karter and his mother were okay. A flurry of thoughts swept through my mind and a numbness ran down my spine. For a moment all my senses left me, and I could no longer hear or see. I could not feel the ground beneath my feet, and I stopped her.

"What do you mean there's been an accident," I questioned.

She said she was on the way to South Carolina from New York and that all she knew was that there was some kind of accident. Karter was fine but Kalen, my other little boy, was on life support.

"It doesn't look good," she whispered so softly it was barely audible.

My entire body went numb and everything around me slowed to a halt. Nothing existed. I did not understand. How could this be? Was I hearing her correctly?

"This doesn't make sense. Was it a car accident? What happened? What hospital?"

I asked these questions, not even consciously thinking about them. Rather, it felt like my mind had taken over and was searching for meaning on its own, a meaning that I could not grasp. She repeated exactly what she just said, only slower. She did not have any real information to share. Before hanging up she gave me the phone number to the hospital's intensive care unit and gave me a special code to give to the ICU nurse. By then, my friends had seen a change in my body and expression and swarmed around, asking questions. I zoned them out completely and dialed the phone number, moving on complete auto pilot. The phone rang only once and a voice on the other side said, "This is the ICU, how can I help you?"

I told the woman my name was Timothy Sherlock, and I was Kalen's father. She asked me to hold, and another woman came on the phone. She apologized that no one from the hospital had called me and asked what I had been told.

"What are you talking about," I demanded. She said, "I don't know how to tell you this. Have you spoken to the investigator?"

Her voice was hesitant and puzzled all at the same time. I wondered why I would need to speak to an investigator.

"No," I replied, "I just got a call that my son was in a car accident and he's on life support." It was all I could muster, anger trembling on my tongue and tears welling behind a dam ready to break free at any moment.

"I don't know how to tell you this," she repeated. "We were under the impression his father was deceased."

Shock set in. Did I just hear this woman correctly? She thought I was dead? Certainly, I wasn't dead. I was talking to her on the phone, and nothing was making any sense at all. The anger was building within me from not knowing, from fear, and from my world spinning out of control like a wayward topsy-turvy toy. I wondered why my ex would give this nurse the impression I was dead. I had just had the boys in New York for a month over the summer and I was on my way to live near them. I was growing frustrated and quickly.

"I am very much alive," I responded. She spoke softly and very measured in an even tone, "Mr. Sherlock, there was no accident. Your son was shot." For the third time in less than an hour the ground fell out from beneath me, my stomach lurched, and acid filled my throat. The sting of the tears meeting the breaking point of the levy that held them at bay pierced my eyes. "I'm sorry," she soothed. "I don't know how else to tell you. Kalen suffered a gun-shot wound to the head."

My entire being came to a crashing halt. Everything inside me shut down. The words that came out of my mouth next seemed to be from another place inside – some detached, clinical, scientific part of my brain that needed to be in control to make it through this moment. It was a built-in survival mechanism that only par-ents could understand. When a child is in danger, a parent of-ten has an autonomic response which allows us to function and protect our children. In that autonomic response I began asking questions.

"Is he brain dead," I spoke into the phone receiver. By now, my friends had gone silent and stood watching. "I can't make that de-termination," she answered. I asked if Kalen was in a coma or re-sponding to any painful stimuli. "For all intents and purposes, he is in a coma and no, he does not respond to those tests," she softly replied. I could hear in this poor woman's' voice the very ache in her heart at having to tell a parent this type of information. "So, you are telling me my son is brain dead," I repeated. "I can't tell you that," she responded.

A tiny sliver of feeling rushed up to the surface, a feeling I knew all too well, red hot rage. "Don't fuck with me," I said to her. "I know enough about science and medicine that everything you are telling me indicates he is brain dead." I just wanted to know the truth. I deserved the truth, the facts, and the probabilities. Why wasn't it like in TV shows and movies where they have all the answers ready for you. She suggested I call the police investigator where I could get more information and provided me with the number. Before we hung up the phone, I asked her one more question. "Ma'am, can you tell me, how long does my son possibly have?" She answered, "That's really anyone's game."

I clicked "end" on the call and hung up the phone. Like a vacuum I could feel everything around me sucked away. Everything was closing in on me. I could feel the very weight of the air leaving my lungs. The world went black. All the noise from the people and traffic and music faded to some distant place I could not access. All I could hear was the most primitive, guttural scream echoing around me and inside me all at once. It was me. I was that primal scream. Something broke in me. I felt it snap and all that was left was this visceral response - a scream that cannot be described by anyone who has not encountered it. It is a scream only created from the very depths of hell and the worst pain and suffering that a human can endure. My soul shattered.

As my senses returned from the world which had collapsed around me, I felt the pressure of someone holding me up. I opened my eyes. I had passed out and fallen to my knees and my friends were holding me, cradling me safely for a brief moment. They voiced a barrage of questions at me wanting to know what just happened, and I simply answered, "I have to go. I have to leave right now. I have to go!" But where was I going? My friend held my face in her hands and looked at me.

"Breathe, Tim, Breathe. We will take you wherever you need to go, but what is going on," she said in the sweetest, most reassuring way. I could see the worry furrowed in the lines on her brow. "Take my phone and call my dad. Find out where he is. I have to go to South Carolina," I said, trying to gather myself and think clearly. I looked her deep in her eyes, and as the levy broke, the tears flooded down my face in a torrent. I feared it would never stop. My throat constricted and filled with all the emotion my body had been holding in. I swallowed, looked her in the eye, and said, "My son is dying!"

As I heard myself speak the words, it felt as if I suddenly realized what happened. It left me raw and stunned. My son was dying. What parent ever says that? This felt unnatural. My mind tried to make sense of it all, but how does the mind make sense of something that isn't supposed to happen, that isn't supposed to exist? As I sat there on the porch, I dialed my father's number. How would I tell him this? Hell, I could not really understand it. Then, once again, my mind and body took over like some type of survival instinct. When he answered I simply asked him where he was and told him I needed to speak to him. He said that he and my mother had just arrived at my aunt's house, following my mom's chemotherapy treatment. He asked me what was going on and I told him I would explain everything when I got there, and I hung up the phone.

The ride to my aunt's house, though a short distance away, felt like an eternity. I kept replaying everything I just heard over and over in my head like a video projector with the reel spinning. Words and images flashed on the big screen of my mind. I kept seeing my little boy's face, my little angel. I saw his smile and the way his eyes glistened when he laughed. Then the words came across the screen: he was shot, in a coma, and on life support. It was all too much to process.

We pulled up and as I walked to the door, I took a steadying breath. In a moment, I would drop a bombshell on my family, the same atom bomb just dropped on me. This news would change, alter, and destroy them on every level, to the very core of their beings. I opened the door and as I entered, I saw my father standing in the doorway to the dining room. My aunt stood by the bathroom door helping my mother out, so she could sit down. My poor mother already showed the effects of her chemotherapy treatment. Frail and unsteady on her feet, her eyes looked glazed over from the heavy medication she had to take.

"Hi baby boy," she said with a smile washing across her face. I could not tell this woman what was happening. She had already been through too much and had so much more to face. I turned to my father, looked him straight in the eye, and steadied myself again. I relayed all the information I learned only minutes earlier. The atmosphere in the room grew dense and heavy. My father pulled out his credit card and said, "Buy a ticket and go." No words were exchanged, except for logistics. No words needed to be said nor were there really any words one could say. My father knew the battle I faced and unconditionally supported me.

My mother sat there, confused, and crying. She caught bits and pieces of what I told my father. "I am going with you; you can't go alone," she kept repeating. This was my sweet mother, seeing her son shattered and broken, doing what a mother does, doing what a parent does. She wanted to protect me and be with me, to ease my pain, and sadly, she knew she couldn't. The same feelings were running through me for my own son Kalen. I told my mother and father I would be fine, that I could handle this. Neither of them liked the idea of me having to do this alone, but this was a journey I had to take myself.

I told my father I would keep him updated on every bit of information I received. I asked if I could have people reach out to him. I did not want to be stuck on the phone reliving and relaying everything I knew to this point with all the family and friends who would want to know. He said he would take care of anything I needed. I packed a bag, kissed my parents and my aunt, and left. My friends had offered to drive me to the airport. I called my ex-mother-in-law and informed her I was on my way. As we settled into the car, my mind began to drift.

SEVEN:
PUSHING THE CLOCK

As THE CAR PULLED away from the curb, two thoughts repeatedly entered my mind: what it means to be a dad, and the fact that I was losing my son – my child, a piece of me. My son Kalen, at only five years old, would never know the joy of being a father himself. He would never bring to reality the boyhood dreams he imagined.

My friend interrupted my thoughts. "Tim, you need to call that investigator," she said, and she was right. I had forgotten, or maybe subconsciously I did not want to call her. I did not want any more information. I did not want to know what was happening. I simply did not want any of it to exist. I wanted to wake up from this hellish dream and return to my happy life and my plans to move to South Carolina and be with my kids.

I ignored those thoughts and reached down to grab my cell phone. This tiny electronic device weighed a million pounds, but

I took a deep breath and did the very thing I did not want to do. I called the investigator whose last name was Valentine. It was déjà vu – reminding me of my earlier call to the ICU. She answered the phone, and I said I was Timothy Sherlock, father of Kalen, and I was told to call her by the nurse at the hospital. "Who," she asked quizzically. I repeated, "I am Timothy Sherlock, and I am Kalen's father." She asked if I could confirm that.

All I could think of doing was to list a litany of facts. I told her that Kalen's birthday was October 11, 2011, and that he was five years old, about to be six. I said he lived in Hartsville, South Carolina with his mother; they moved there approximately two years ago. Kalen was born in a hospital in Canandaigua, New York and he weighed six pounds and 11 ounces and was 21 and a quarter inches long.

"Well, okay," she responded, "What do you know?" I told Ms. Valentine I knew nothing other than the fact that my son was shot in the head, and I spurted, "How in the fuck was he shot in the head? Was he playing with a gun? Was it an accident?" The words that followed stunned me to the core. "Oh, Mr. Sherlock," she said, "at this point we are treating this as intentional." She explained that until more information came, it appeared that this was not an accident. All I could think was, who the fuck shot my son?

Ms. Valentine explained that, from her understanding, my ex-wife's boyfriend pulled the trigger. She said she could not provide all the details yet, because the investigation just started. However, she confirmed that the police received a call at 3:30 a.m. stating that Kalen's mother had taken him from their home to the nearest hospital instead of calling 911. They put Kalen on a helicopter and moved him from the hospital of arrival to McLeod, near Darlington, South Carolina. She said she would call me back and give me all the details she had after her next meeting. I provided my telephone number and hung up the phone.

I stared out the window, the phone in my hand. The world outside rushed past as we drove, inching closer to the hell I would soon face. "Why is time moving so fast," I thought to myself. Didn't time realize I needed it to slow down? I needed more of it. I needed more time.

The information from Investigator Valentine spun through my head. As my brain tried to comprehend it, a million more questions arose with no answers. How am I supposed to make any sense of this, I wondered. A father is supposed to die before his child. I am supposed to go first.

I looked at the front seat to see my friend looking back at me, her eyes wanting to know what I just learned. She wanted to help and looked lost and confused. She didn't know how to help me. No one did. How do you help someone going through something like this? These horrors only happen on the news or in movies, not in our own lives. Yet, there I was, and everything seemed to be happening all too quickly. I could offer her no words. I simply stared back into her eyes, wishing she could take my hurt away. I wished it was all a bad dream. Staring back at her, I said the only thing that came to mind: "Murder!" No other words would come out. I spoke it and turned my attention back to the window and time lunged forward at breakneck speed.

The road created a steady pulse in the car, as the tires passed over paved expressway. A mantra repeated over and over in my mind: "God please, God please, God please." I focused on the sound of the drive and numbness settled in. My mind eased into a happier place and time. Images of my son's face streamed into my consciousness. I saw him smiling with those shining, bright, chestnut eyes that have a hint of honey around the rim. I saw his cherub cheeks as he smiled and laughed.

For a moment, I could smell his sweet child scent and feel the softness of his youthful skin. I could hear the timber of his laugh, like church bells in a distant valley on a bright day. The tears streamed silently down my face and along the crevices of my skin, collecting, and dripping into my lap. Those silent tears were full of the heaviness of the universe. It felt like all of creation cried with me. Before I knew it, the car slowed, and at once, pulled me from nothingness. This leg of my journey ended and a new one would begin. I took a steadying breath and with all my soul could muster, I prayed to God. "Just give me time to get there, please."

EIGHT:
LET THIS BE HEAVEN

We arrived at the Buffalo International Airport and my friend walked me inside. As I approached the kiosk, she went the other way and disappeared. I checked in and turned around to find myself standing face to face with a security guard.

"Hello," he said. "Your friend told me what was going on. I am going to escort you. I am a father myself. I can't imagine…"

I asked him to please stop talking. I could not handle pity or platitude. Though I knew his heart ached for me, my being could not process it. I was a broken man on a mission. I needed to follow this path without interruption. At the terminal, the staff had called ahead, and a stewardess awaited me. She asked me to sit down and told me not to move; that they would get me on the plane. Everyone handled me gently. I could see my own fear in their eyes

– the fear that I might break or shatter. Each person I encountered looked at me with such pity. Their eyes spoke words they could not say aloud: "This poor, poor man."

Though intellectually I felt thankful for the assistance and kindness, I never have been someone who likes to be catered to. I do not enjoy being treated as if I am weak. Gentle felt safe, but I did not want comfort. It took all my effort to balance my psyche between total dissociation and profound emotional torture.

Again, my phone rang, and it filled me with dread. I looked at the caller ID and realized it was the investigator. I hesitantly answered, preparing for more bad news and more unanswered questions. The investigator told me she had additional information about the night Kalen was shot, and in regard to my other son Karter. I took a deep breath and listened.

She began, "Karter was home watching television when the police arrived, and the boyfriend was hiding in a field. He had put the gun in a lunch box and was trying to bury it." She went on to say, Karter was placed in emergency foster care because there was no one to place him with. She reassured me he was doing fine. I asked why his mother didn't have him. She explained that his mother was under investigation as well. "There is a lot to this," Ms. Valentine explained. "I need to speak to you when you arrive. When will you be in town?"

I told her my plane would leave at 4:00 p.m. and I should arrive around 6:30. She apologized, and I apologized back. I asked if I could contact her as soon as my plane landed, but she preferred to contact me instead. She said she wanted to meet with me after I had time with my son. I thanked her and as I hung up the phone, the stewardess approached me. It was time to board the plane.

The stewardess moved me into first class, in the seat right next to her by a window. A gentleman sat in our row in the aisle seat. The stewardess disappeared, reappeared, and reached out her hand. She held out a small bottle of whiskey. I just found out my son got shot and this woman unknowingly offered me the one thing she thought, and I knew, would numb the pain. I had enough sobriety to know that bottle would make all this worse. I looked at her directly in the eyes and said, "No, ma'am, I do not drink. I am an alcoholic. I cannot drink." "I just wanted to help," she said.

In that moment I needed one thing – to get to my son. I felt the weight of eyes on me. It seemed like every person near me stared, as if they knew. Could they read my energy? Could they see this man balancing between heaven and hell, on the verge of complete devastation? Of course, they couldn't, but I still felt like a specimen under a microscope.

The stranger in the aisle seat tried to make small talk and I ignored him completely. I had nothing to say. Would he even want to talk to me if he knew? Would he say the same words if he understood my heart had shattered? The questions in my mind seemed endless.

Finally, the plane rose into the sky and soon we floated in that magical in-between space. I could see the top of the clouds; the oranges, pinks, and yellows bouncing off the puffy white; the hazy blue of the horizon and the darker sky above. I stared at the beauty out my window, and it overtook me. I started crying.

Kalen would die and no miracle could save him. This view felt as close as I could get to heaven. It became the heaven I wanted for my son – pure beauty. I knew only God could create such a sight, but I could not be part of it. Looking upon it from the window of my plane would be as close as I could get. Kalen would soon go somewhere I could not follow, at least not for now.

I asked God, right there in the clouds, to give me time with my son; to hold him while his heart was still beating. I knew praying for survival was pointless. Everything I heard and all my intuition told me, Kalen was terminal. Looking out of the window into the clouds, I asked for time. I needed to say goodbye. I needed to tell him I was sorry. I pleaded, "God, please let this be heaven. Let this be what he sees when he dies because it is so beautiful." Kalen deserved that.

The man in the aisle seat asked me if I was okay. I told him. "I'm on the way to South Carolina to see my son. He is dying." The man responded kindly, "Can I ask how old?" I told him Kalen was five. He said he had a grandson that age. I remember thinking this isn't right. FIVE. You are not supposed to die when you are five years old. Your biggest worry should be, "What G.I. Joe should I play with," or, "Can I sneak a snack out of the cupboard before mom sees?" He should not be fighting for his life, I thought.

Exhausted and drained, my mind grew ever wearier. Then, just like that, it hit me – how deeply I let my son down. I thought of all the things I never taught him and the moments he would never experience. I failed to protect him and now he was fighting for his life. As parents, we teach our children not to be afraid. We teach them there is no monster under the bed at night. We teach them that spiders won't hurt them, and a bee won't sting if you don't provoke it. We teach them the necessary things like the danger of the road, sharp objects, and of course strangers.

I thought back to a conversation we had. I told Kalen monsters did not exist; that the evil, scary things he feared in his room and home were not real. I told him home was safe. What a lie! I never had a chance to teach him monsters are real or that danger does exist in the people we trust. I never told him, nor did I believe I would have to, that sometimes those we love and trust the most are the monsters we should really fear. I always thought these were lessons he would grow to learn. I thought we had time - all the time in the world, a lifetime. Now doctors measured Kalen's time in heart beats, like sand falling through an hourglass. He would soon run out. My son, my baby, my miracle, my gift. I sat back in my seat in first-class and sunk into the memories – floating in a place in my mind where I could remember safety and happiness.

I don't know how much time passed. The voice of the flight attendant over the speaker pulled me away from my life as it flashed through my mind. She instructed us to place our tray tables in the upright position as we circled for landing. Despite the interruption I went right back into the movie of my life. It seemed so fast. Life moved far too quickly. The questions returned. How could this be happening? How could I come so far only to be cut down now? I felt the urgency to be with my sons – both of them. The questions quickened like a roller coaster roaring down a track full of twists, turns, and loops. My stomach became queasy, and my head felt disoriented.

NINE:
TRUTH BE TOLD

I STEPPED OFF THE plane in South Carolina, gathered myself and my thoughts, and called my former mother-in-law. I told her I landed, and she asked if I knew anything more. She still seemed unsure what had happened. I shared what the investigator told me and said I needed someone to pick me up at the airport and take me to the hospital. I hung up the phone and immediately my phone rang again. It was the investigator. She had questions too. As the conversation ensued a clearer picture began to emerge.

Ms. Valentine asked if my ex-wife took drugs or drank alcohol. I explained that she appeared to be a heavy drinker, that I was in recovery, and that I had often wanted my ex-wife to quit drinking as well. I asked why she asked such a question. She explained that marijuana residue and signs of alcohol and drug use appeared in the home where Kalen was shot. "Mr. Sherlock, were you aware the boyfriend was on a probation and not allowed to own a firearm?" I felt stunned. Apparently, he pulled a gun on a woman a few years earlier and after being charged with menacing, the system put him on probation. I started feeling extremely agitated and insisted Ms. Valentine explain what was happening. "From the information I am gathering, the boyfriend is admitting he shot Kalen." Likely in shock himself, he just kept repeating, "I did it. I did it. I did it."

While the details continued to emerge, none of it made sense to me. My mind struggled to paint the full picture. I asked about my ex-wife. Ms. Valentine explained, she went in for questioning and then to the hospital. "Questioning for what," I demanded. The investigator told me after Kalen got shot, she left to take him to the hospital but never called 911. Instead, she called her boyfriend 15 times.

My mind swirled with the kinds of questions no one could or would answer for me. Had there been physical abuse in the home? Was there abuse between or upon her and the children? I always thought those things were possibilities but never had evidence. I continued to question why the investigator or hospital hadn't called me first and she explained, my ex made it very clear, I was not in the picture, and she had no contact information for me. All the while, I had gotten sober and was actively enacting a plan with my ex-wife to move there. I thought back to when she first took them from New York to South Carolina. I called every single day in the beginning. When those calls went unanswered, I called weekly. I would call and call – text and text – and maybe once a month someone responded. For me, it just wasn't enough. While I loved the month I had with my boys over the summer, I needed more time.

As the investigator wrapped up our call, I remembered that back in my apartment in Wellsville, a teddy bear still lay where Kalen slept. Some of his dirty clothes littered the floor. The month my boys just spent with me was picture perfect. Every single morning, I woke up and made pancakes or eggs and bacon. After we ate, the boys watched cartoons or played with toys while I cleaned up and took the dogs outside. Twice a week, we packed a picnic lunch and went to the park to explore the river, catch fish, and play with tadpoles. We had adventures – like going to the library to pick out books and put tickets in the auction for the reading program. We participated in a dog toy drive for the SPCA – braiding pieces of fleece fabric into little knots for dog pulls.

We attended the Hot Air Balloon Rally and went on walks every day. I had not started driving yet, so we hopped on the bus and went to my hometown to visit family. Every night, we ate dinner together; sometimes my sponsor would join us. My friend Michelle, who handmade the urn that holds Kalen's ashes, would babysit on Tuesday and Wednesday nights so I could attend my AA meetings. On Sunday, a friend would pick us up and take us to an early morning meeting. We built forts, conducted science experiments, ran through the garden paths, and picked the raspberries I planted the year before. There were typical sibling arguments and little kid temper tantrums – but even those gave me joy.

In one vivid moment, Karter sat on the couch watching television and coloring, the dogs wrapped up around him. "Where is your brother," I asked. "I don't know," he answered. I looked out of the little window above the countertop in the kitchen and there was Kalen, sitting on the roots of a tree, feeding his freezie pop to one of the dogs. I called out, "What are you doing?" He had this huge smile on this face and laughed, "Oh nothing, just sitting here." He was so goofy. I watched him eating his popsicle in the sunlight without a care in the world, petting the dog, and I thought, my God, I am so lucky.

I needed more of it and felt extremely excited to move to South Carolina. I told my sponsor that night, I was so grateful for my recovery and for those kids. An overwhelming joy filled my heart. That Sunday we went to a meeting and Kalen drew a picture of the three of us with mohawks on our heads. It still hangs in my house. That Monday the boys left. I gave Kalen a big hug and a kiss, and he said, "Dee Dee, I'm going to see you soon, right?" "You are going to see me really soon," I answered, and they pulled out of the driveway.

Now, I faced a visit I never imagined. The investigator told me information that shook me to my core. I promised to go to her office the next day to talk more. As soon as that call ended, my phone rang again. My ex-mother-in-law greeted me. She said someone would be at the airport to pick me up. Then, she spoke tentatively into the receiver. "Apparently, her boyfriend had the gun," she said. I told her I knew that and already spoke at length with the investigator. She instructed me to watch for a man with a sign, who would be waiting outside the airport to pick me up. Perhaps the hospital sent someone to get me, I thought.

When I walked out, a man stood nearby holding a sign with my name on it, just like she said. He introduced himself by his first name. I grabbed my things, and we loaded them into the car. "I am really sorry, by the way," he said. "We are praying." Clearly, this stranger knew why I was there and what was happening with my son. "Who are you again," I asked. He explained who he was – the father of my ex-wife's boyfriend. Something happened inside me.

TEN:
A DESCENT INTO HELL

WHAT DID THIS MAN just say to me? Did he honestly just introduce himself as the father of the man who shot my son, who killed my son? A sense of rage swelled in me like nothing I had ever felt before. Fire flashed behind my eyes, and everything seemed to be bathed in a red glow. A heat arose along my neck. I wanted to scream and hit and punch. I wanted this man to hurt, and why? I had no clue. Almost instantly, a flash of white replaced the red and all my mind could see was my baby boy, smiling and laughing. I knew that, for now, I had to remain calm.

This man standing here had nothing to do with what was happening. I took a deep breath and gathered myself, letting go of the anger, and thought of my Kalen. I visualized him growing up, holding him, rocking him, and teaching him how to walk. No matter what, Kalen always wore a smile on his face. He emanated pure joy, and he loved people. He truly was the most angelic baby I had ever seen. He also had a mischievous but inquisitive personality that balanced out his sweetness.

He always wanted to know how the world worked and what made people tick. He loved to make people laugh and push you right to the edge with a barrage of questions without crossing that imaginary line. He was content and full of excitement – always with a story to tell or a joke to share. He constantly teased me. "Don't trip!" he would say, "Your flip flops are untied," or "Look, you lost your pocket!"

As we drove to the hospital I sat quietly. I had no intention of making small talk with this man. All we shared that day was our names and his apology. He talked and I listened, and I liked it that way. He went on about how much they loved Kalen, and how he truly was a part of their family. I knew this man was hurting, and I knew he was uncomfortable, but I also knew that if I said anything I would lose myself and take it out on him. He had nothing to do with why I was sitting in this car, and my anger would serve no purpose on this journey. No, I needed to remain quiet and strong.

As we arrived at the hospital, I felt overwhelmed by the enormous size of it. I learned it was the largest hospital in the state, and the largest employer. I could not get over its beauty and enormity. The campus included many buildings, each with a different job to do. The children's center stood large, with an exterior made of a wall of glass. It reminded me of a huge hotel, inviting and beautiful; but I knew it was not a hotel. I knew exactly what was on the other side of the glass door - pure sorrow. We made our way in, and to a set of elevators, bringing us up, up, and away.

The Intensive Care Unit took up a whole floor and looked prestigious, with seating and waiting areas, a long hall with glass on one side, and a row of large, solid wood doors. Each door was adorned with its own keypad entry system. As we walked down this hall, I knew that one of these doors held my son within it. We stopped about halfway down the hallway, and he turned to ask me if I had the code. I shook my head. He gave me the code, then punched it in himself. I breathed the deepest breath I could, steadied myself, and entered the belly of the beast. There was no turning back now.

As I walked into the hospital room where his body lay, I could barely recognize my Kalen. My eyes registered the scene and sent messages to my brain. It did not look like what you see in television shows or movies. This was not my son. It couldn't be. They clearly had the wrong child, or we walked into the wrong room. He looked so tiny; too little for the bed cradling his sleeping body. The covers tucked up to his chin hid his frame, revealing only his small round face, now puffy and swollen. A ventilator tube held his delicate lips agape – the ones that told me jokes and called me Dee Dee, the ones that asked a thousand questions.

Machines blinked and beeped nearby. Bandages had been carefully wrapped around his head at an angle covering one eye like something you see in a war encampment. But he was not a man; not a soldier struck down on the front line of battle. He was Kalen - my little boy; my five-year-old son. His other eye was swollen, puffy, and discolored. They later explained this was caused by the ventilator. There were wires coming from every direction, out of every possible area of him. No, this was not my son. My son was strong and healthy and smiling. My son had muscles and was a big boy. He wasn't this little boy, this tiny child being engulfed by a sea of medical equipment, hanging on the very edge of life and death.

The tears ran out of my eyes, along the ridge of my nose, and down my face. They spilled over the blanket now keeping my son warm. Each tear swelled with all the hurt and all the torture I felt. Each tear was a piece of my soul leaving my body. This image would haunt me far longer than any other trauma in my entire life. It would rip me apart at the seams, scattering the pieces of me to the floor in disarray like a puzzle that could never be put back together. I would have to build a new picture, an abstract, from the pieces left behind. Perhaps therein lies the gift of a child, to understand the beauty life has to offer - not the pre-scripted pattern laid out but rather, what we create from chaos. Isn't the birth process chaotic? Human life is chaotic. Kalen taught me to see the beauty in it all; to look through his eyes and know what it means to be purely innocent; to see the world my son saw. Children give us far more than we give them.

As I looked around the room, for reassurance and for someone to tell me it was going to be okay, it never came. Instead, I realized for the first time, the room was full of people - strange people I did not recognize other than my ex-mother-in-law and my ex-wife. I was introduced to the family of the man who shot my son. Again, like a surge of red-hot fire, I was engulfed in anger. These people did not belong here. This was not his family. This was the family of the man that put my baby here. Seeing Kalen I knew, this should be a private moment.

I wanted to scream and yell and kick them all out. It all felt so unfair; they did not deserve to be there. Then, just like before, the anger pumping through my veins gave way to another sensa-tion. Out of nowhere, an image entered my mind accompanied by a thought: this was the family my son knew while he lived here. These were the people he spent time with and the people that loved him as much as I loved him, just in a different way. I stuffed my anger away, as I had been stuffing so many feelings over the last few hours. I placed it somewhere in the back of my brain to be dealt with later. I turned and looked back at my son - my small helpless son.

I moved to the side of his bed, wedging myself between it and the wall. I needed to put distance between myself and the people in the room. At the same time, I needed to be near Kalen, as close to him as I could be. I reached under the blanket, surprised by how warm the bed was. I noticed that his blanket was inflated, filled with warm air cycling through it. The nurse explained this was to help keep him warm as his body was not regulating its own temperature, and that his organs were slowly shutting down. I grabbed my son's tiny hand and held it in mine. Was his hand always this tiny? I tried to think back, and in my mind, I remembered it being so much larger. Now, however, it was tiny, and I covered it with my own. I prayed to God for Kalen to hear me.

"Kalen, it's Dee Dee. I'm here buddy," I told him between sobs. "I am here, and you are okay buddy. Dee Dee is so sorry buddy."

In the swollen, puffy, discolored face of my son, I searched for the boy I had seen only a few weeks ago. I looked for a hint of his smile, the curve of his lips, anything. I pulled forward a memory of playing hide and seek with him. Then, through my tears, I noticed something on his face. The nurse stood nearby, and I told her that I needed a tissue. When she asked what for, I said, "I have to wipe his nose." A little piece of mucous protruded out. The nurse explained that it was not a booger on his nose. It was his brain, dissolving. The room shrunk and the sounds of the machines seemed suddenly louder. The world stopped moving for a moment. Nothing else existed that was real except me and Kalen, father and son. I knew what needed to be done and I would tend to every detail.

She moved toward Kalen, and I stopped her. "You are not touching my son," I said, with absolute authority. "I am his father. I have to take care of him." The nurse explained that she needed everyone to leave the room; that she needed to clean him and change the bandages. I was not leaving. I had only just gotten here. I was not and would not be leaving my son. By now the doctor walked in. He explained to me that it was not their protocol to allow the parents in the room during such procedures. I explained to him that I understood what he was doing, and that I would either be assisting them, or they would be removing me with force.

"Let him unwrap his head," the doctor told the nurse. Kalen was dying and this was our time. The doctor understood. He explained to me what to expect, and that he did not recommend doing this. He explained that they were worried about infection and that I would have to gown up and use the protective equipment. I told the doctor I understood his concerns, but I would do this, and nothing could change my mind.

I carefully pulled the bandages away from Kalen's face and skull. A large hole above his eye next to his temple marked the bullet's exit point. The exit wound was much larger than the entry wound on the back of his head. Bone and brain shown through the hole. I flushed and packed the wound before carefully rewrapping his tiny little head. I was not allowed to break down; it was my job to take care of him. I did not understand at the time the impact seeing him this way would have on me. For a year, whenever I thought of Kalen, the wound was all I could see. I battled that trauma through therapy and recovery.

Now, cleaned up and rebandaged, Kalen's life would be measured in minutes. To me, each minute was a decade in slow motion. I talked to my son, as I battled my own internal struggle. Maybe you should be afraid of the people you love, I thought. The man he loved and called dad – one of his best friends - did this to him. Even though he was in a coma I felt I needed to soothe him. I wanted to show him people could be good; not all people are monsters. I wanted him to know that his father loved him and would take care of him.

ELEVEN:
GOODBYE MY BOY

I LOOKED AT MY son, now all cleaned up and bandaged, but still lifeless. Suddenly, I couldn't breathe, and I needed air. I reached for my cigarettes and silently excused myself from the room. I needed space to get as far away as possible from the reality before me. I walked outside, lit a cigarette, and called my dad to update him. The call lasted only moments, but I could hear the exhaustion and helplessness in his voice. I knew what he was feeling for the first time in my life. I could understand what he was going through as a father. The helplessness he felt for me, his son, was the same helplessness I felt as a father for my son.

I sat on the curb enjoying the lack of chaos for a moment, focusing only on my breathing and the cigarette. I could hear the cars and people talking, and decided to walk for a bit, away from this fortress of death that became my new reality. As I walked, I could see a bar off in the distance, and the thought of a drink crossed my mind. I knew someone in that bar probably had drugs and I could escape all of this. I stood there, tempted by oblivion, but instead I reached for my phone and called my sponsor. I knew that no drug was going to fix this, that I was going to have to face reality, and be there for my son. After my phone call, I made my way back, knowing my son needed me. Decisions needed to be made. I wanted to see Karter and I wanted him to see his brother.

It was an excruciating decision to allow Karter to come and see his brother in the hospital. People may argue vehemently on either side, but I felt Karter had the right to be with us. I argued about it with my ex-wife and her family, but I held my ground. The CPS investigator stopped by and indicated there would be strict ground rules for the visit. First, it had to be supervised. CPS had not yet established me as the father and the investigator shared that my ex was not allowed to be alone with the kids. The realization sunk in deeper that they were looking at her as part of the investigation.

Meanwhile, as the day went on, people came and went from the room. One constant was that my ex-wife's phone kept ringing. "Who the hell keeps calling," I asked in frustration. I just wanted the time with Kalen to be quiet and peaceful. Her mom said that it was him – the man who shot my son. He had been calling every couple of hours. After one such call, my ex turned and asked if he could speak to Kalen. The representative from Child Protective Services said, "Absolutely not," and informed her that he was to have no contact. They also reiterated that she was to have no more direct contact with him and reported it to the police investigator.

I could not believe my ears. Had she just asked if the man who did this to my son could talk to him? This monster took my son, and she wanted to give him the chance to speak to Kalen? What the fuck? How could she even be talking to him at all? The rage surged again in me, and as I looked at my ex, I saw her as a monster in that moment. Red hot piercing contempt arose in me. I wanted to scream and hit and fight once again. Instead, I walked away. I allowed the CPS investigator to handle the situation. My anger, for now, would only add to this nightmare.

In those first hours after my arrival, when the doctor left and my ex-wife came in, I asked her a direct question. "How does this even happen," I said, "You grew up in a hunting family. You know gun safety better than anyone. Who puts a gun under a sink or keeps a loaded gun in the house?" She just kept repeating, "I don't know; I don't know." She said, "I was sleeping. I don't know how it happened. He said it was an accident. I believe him. He loved those boys." As my suspicions escalated, questions erupted in spurts. I wondered why in the hell I still could not be left alone with my son. I wanted to know what happened between her and that man. Why did the police, CPS, and the hospital think I was dead? I wanted answers about Kalen. I wanted answers to questions I had already asked.

The hospital staff told me the first 24 hours after an injury like Kalen suffered are crucial and that kids are weird; they can bounce back from the strangest things. After 24 hours the doctors would run a test and, by state law, would run the test twice to determine if there was any brain activity. Meanwhile, the hospital staff simply treated what was presented to them. The only advice they had was to spend as much time with my son as possible. I never left Kalen's side from my arrival to his passing except to walk outside for a cigarette. Looking around at everyone in and out of the room I did not know what to say or think. My boy lay in a bed dying. I knew that in my heart, yet no one had a clear picture for me. At one point, I walked out of the room and back in. Everyone had left. I sat down on the bedside and talked to my son alone.

"Hey buddy, how are you doing?" I asked. "I hope you can hear me. I love you so, so, so much. It's okay, Kalen. You don't have to fight. If this hurts you, you can leave. Daddy will be okay." I told him all about the day he came into the world, how I held him, and how happy I felt. I told him I was honored to be his father and I thanked him for all the joy he had given to me.

The nurse saw me with Kalen and asked if I was okay. "I just don't get it," I told her. "I'm not a bad person. I've never done anything in my life that deserves being punished like this. Kalen doesn't deserve this." The emotions rose to the surface once again and like Sally Fields in Steel Magnolias I just screamed out, "Why?!" The nurse rubbed my back until I calmed down. I apologized and her eyes widened. She said, "No! You do not apologize for anything. I have a five-year-old at home. I cannot imagine what you are going through right now." I told her I just wanted him to come back – for twenty minutes; hell, for two minutes. But he wasn't coming back. There was nothing she could do except comfort me. She went to get me an ice water, sensing I needed a moment, and doing all she could think of to bring me comfort.

My ex-wife and her mom returned to the room, and they took the pull-out couch so they could sleep. They went to bed as I sat in a chair, praying to God, trying to make sense of what was happening. I kept asking God to forgive me and saying how sorry I was for not protecting Kalen. I apologized for not fighting harder to get him to New York permanently. I apologized for every time I ever used a drug or drank alcohol. I begged him to lay down this burden. Hours must have passed because when I got up to go the bathroom, the sun was rising outside the window. I'd been awake all night. Rachel, the night nurse, was getting ready to end her shift and I asked if there was a place for me to get a large cup of coffee. "Absolutely honey," she answered, "There's a Starbucks downstairs." I gave her my cell phone number and asked her to please call me if Kalen woke up.

Tears filled her eyes. "Honey, I don't think Kalen is going to wake up," she whispered. It was the first time anyone had been honest with me. I looked at her and I said, "I know." I picked up my things and went downstairs. Coffee in hand, I made my way to the courtyard where a fountain splashed water down onto the ground. The light reflected off the water as the sun rose. The water disappeared under the ground, and I sat there thinking. I could see Kalen playing in the water and me responding, "You better get out of there or you are going to get in trouble!" He would shoot back a half-cocked smile and put his toe in the water anyway. That was my son in my mind, not the boy laying in that bed fighting for his life, a life I knew he would never actually live. I realized my memories and imagination were all I would have left of him.

My heart wrenched and I pleaded, "God, please take me instead. I will gladly die. Just let him live." I didn't care if he was handicapped or disabled; he just needed more time. I called my sponsor to talk and remembered, in my exhaustion, I had spoken with her throughout the night as well. She called every couple of hours to check in on me. I spoke with my cousin who had gotten in very late in the night and had gone to a hotel. She was going to be coming to the hospital later this afternoon. At least I wouldn't be totally alone in this.

As I made my way back to the room, my ex-wife and her mother were just waking up and they brought breakfast in. I couldn't bring myself to eat. The nurse arrived and indicated they would soon be running the test and the doctors would make their rounds. Life just moved on normally around us. We were here, stuck, and life proceeded as usual - each person fulfilling their roles and duties. Didn't they understand that there was nothing normal about this? Didn't they understand that a child was dying and so was his father?

A social worker came to facilitate Karter's visit and coordinate with the nurse and CPS. I could be with him in a playroom down the hall. The doctors would be running the first set of tests on Kalen as CPS walked me through everything we needed to do to facilitate Karter's arrival. They talked about how they would cover Kalen up so that Karter would not be traumatized by the visual appearance of his brother, which would allow him some closure without further harming him. I agreed this was the best approach, as I didn't want to cause any more harm to Karter or make the situation any worse than it could be, if that was even possible.

The CPS worker and the hospital staff left to prepare for Karter's arrival and I made my way back to Kalen's room with my ex-wife. A line of workers stood along the wall. I saw them and thought, is this a firing range? A man approached me and said, "I am Dr. Gomez, the chief pediatric neurologist." He told me that in South Carolina, they unhook the machine and read whether the patient breaths on their own and has brain waves. He told me that Kalen did not pass the test. He kept apologizing and in his next breath, with no emotion, as if he were reading out of a textbook, he delivered a crushing blow.

He said the little boy I knew no longer existed and if he were to make it through this, he would live his life in a wheelchair as a vegetable. The words screamed out in my mind, "Oh my God, my son is gone. The doctor just said it. Where did my little boy go?" I could see his body; it was right there, but everything that made him Kalen was gone. I would never hear another knock-knock joke, watch him flex his muscles, catch another polliwog, or climb another rock together. If he lived, he would spend this life suffering. This was not the life he was meant to live; this is not what was supposed to happen. "Can we pull the plug," I asked.

"Mr. Sherlock, you are jumping the fence here," the doctor said. I told him, I didn't want to put Kalen through this anymore. The doctor said he had to run the test a second time by law. My ex-wife appeared to go numb, staring at the doctor's, void of any emotions. Tears streamed down my face and down the faces of the nurses and my ex-mother-in-law, but my ex stood there as if someone just told her the weather. I felt so angry and so hurt. I lashed out. I grabbed my cigarettes, looked at my ex square in the eyes and said, "You did this. I will never forgive you," and I stormed out.

As I walked downstairs to smoke, a strange light caught my eye and I turned to see a room with a piano and the most beautiful stained glass. I peeked my head in and realized it was the hospital chapel. I walked to the front of the room and kneeled, looking up at the sign of the cross. If God was there, he would hear me now. "I hate you," I said, "I hate you. How dare you? If you are such a benevolent and loving God, why would you take my child? Give him back! He is not yours. He is mine! Give him back." The tears flowed from my eyes as I sat still, crying.

Slowly and gradually as the pain came out, the hairs on the back of my neck stood up. A feeling of peace permeated my whole body. A thought entered my mind in the form of an image. He was never yours, Tim. He was always God's. I looked back up at the cross and I said, "Just keep him safe. Don't let him feel any pain. Don't let him suffer. Give him a beautiful life up there."

Just then, a pastor walked in and asked if he could help me with anything. I said, "No, you can't," and I left. Back upstairs, the time had finally arrived for Karter's visit and the nurse walked me to the playroom. My ex-wife's aunt had flown in from Massachusetts by then, and my cousin was in route. We made our way down to the playroom and waited for my oldest son to show up. The nurse showed us what she had done to help Karter with his visit with Kalen. She showed us the hat she put on Kalen's head to hide the bandages. She color coded every tube so they could answer all of Karter's questions, should he have any. She explained, "We will talk to him first in the playroom, visit with him and spend a little time together, and then move to the hospital room when we are ready." She asked if I had any questions and I said, "No, I will lean on you and your expertise."

TWELVE:
A 7-YEAR-OLD WITNESS

THE HOSPITAL PLAYROOM LOOKED more like an oversized game room. It featured a foosball table, an air hockey table, and every toy imaginable for every child. The room offered every bit of fun that could be imagined. I wandered that cavernous room, while my ex-wife and her family sat at a small table in the corner talking. They paid me no attention nor did I them. I wandered around the room, thinking of what games I could play with my son. I hadn't seen Karter in just over a month, but even that seemed like a lifetime given all the changes of the last 24 hours.

The sound of the door opening made me spin around, and there was my amazing son - the other half of my two. "Dee Dee," he yelled and came running to me. I scooped him up into the biggest hug I could muster, and in that moment all my sadness washed away. All the worry and weight lifted, and I felt whole.

He ran over and very briefly hugged his mom. Even I could notice how tentative and timid he was. He said hello to his grandmother and aunt, then came right back to me. I asked him how he was doing, and how it was where he was staying. I told him how much I missed him. We explored the room, looking to see what we would do first as he told me about his foster home. He said he liked it. He told me they were very nice, and that they had chickens and a trampoline. Other kids lived there too, who he could play with. He then asked when he was coming home. I told him it was going to be a little bit, and that he needed to stay there, so that mommy and daddy could tend to his brother. He looked up at me with those big, beautiful brown eyes. Just like his brother's, they had a touch of honey around the edges. Now they looked wide and scared. I brought him over to a spot on the floor and sat him on my lap.

"Karter", I asked, "Do you know what happened and why we are here?" He snuggled onto my lap, pushing his body into mine as he did when he was younger, looking for comfort. In the smallest of voices, he answered yes. I asked him, "What do you remember, Karter? What do you know about what happened?" I gauged his response as a guide for what to say next. What was too much to tell him, I wondered, and how much would he understand?

In that moment my little boy seemed to age and grow into an adult in a matter of moments, and I could see his childhood innocence vanishing in an instant. We sat there in silence for a moment, just father and son - my buddy and me. I listened to his breathing and felt the weight of him in my lap. The touch of his skin grounded me in the realness of the moment. He was here. My son was in my arms, and I could hold him. This became the first real thing to me, through all I had just been through. I waited a moment and bent down to say he could tell me anything. I also said if he didn't want to talk, that was fine.

He leaned into me closer and began to speak about that night. He said he had been sleeping, then he just woke up. He said he woke up scared, and his heart was racing but he didn't know why. Yet, he knew there was something scary in the house. He told me he could hear mommy and her boyfriend yelling, but he didn't know what they were saying. He ran to Kalen's room because Kalen was probably scared too, but when he got there, Kalen wasn't in his bed, so he ran to the living room. He said that mommy was running out the door.

Karter told me he ran up to mommy's boyfriend and asked where she was going. The man responded by asking Karter what he was doing there, and why mom left him. Karter told me he got up onto the couch and mom's boyfriend gave him a blanket and turned on the television. He sat there while the man ran around the house going through the cupboards, and he grabbed Kalen's lunch pail. He then went over to Karter and said he was sorry, he didn't mean to shoot his brother. He turned and went outside. In the midst of telling me the story, Karter stopped for a moment and took a breath. I sat with him. I knew he would go on when he was ready, but I asked, what happened next? He said he got up and went to look for Kalen. He walked into Kalen's room and turned on the light. He said it was scary in there. I would later learn what he had seen when he turned on those lights.

Karter continued, he went back to the couch and covered up in the blanket. Then, there was a knock on the door. A policeman came in, and he could see all the lights flashing outside. He could hear dogs barking. He said the policeman asked him if anyone else was home and he shook his head no. He said the policeman asked if he was okay, and he said yes. He was watching tv and mommy left; mommy's boyfriend left, and he didn't know where his brother was. He said the policeman walked through the house and then sat with him and told him that someone was coming to pick him up.

Karter asked the policeman if I was picking him up, but he said no, it was a nice lady who was going to take him someplace safe. He said a lady came in and asked him a bunch of questions and then told him that his brother was hurt really bad. She said he was going to stay with a friend of the ladies for a little while, until they figured out what happened. He told me that the nice lady told him about foster care, and she helped him wrap up in the blanket. They left and went to his new home.

Karter then paused again. He looked up at me and said, I heard them talking – the foster lady and the CPS lady. They said something about Kalen being shot. He looked me deep in the eyes and asked "Dee Dee, was Kalen shot?" That question hit me to the core. How was I supposed to do this, to tell him? How do you explain these things? I felt like I had to navigate so many unknown paths in such a short time, traversing each moment alone with no guidance. How do parents deal with situations like this, I wondered. How do I answer him? I squeezed him tight into me, readied my breath, and answered as honestly and simply as I could.

"Yes, he was shot. Do you know what that means?" I asked. He shook his head and without looking back at me, asked me where Kalen was shot. "In his head buddy." "Oh, that is bad. Will he be okay?" my son asked. I told him I did not know, but the doctors were doing everything they could do to fix him. I asked if he wanted to see his brother. My son sat silently for a moment and asked if we could just maybe play for a while and see him after. Of course, we could. I wasn't going to force my son to go through anything he didn't want to. This had to be on his terms, and I had to follow his lead. It felt nice not to have to make any decisions for a moment.

I nestled into my son closely, tussling his hair, and noticed how long it had gotten. Jokingly, I asked him if he wanted to get a haircut. Maybe we could leave the hospital for a little while. As I did so, I noticed something moving in his hair. I looked closer and asked if his head itched. He looked at me and said yes, all the time. I looked up at my wife and asked her to come over. She informed me he had lice. She said she hadn't gotten around to treating it, then forgot. I felt dumbfounded. It seemed there was no end to the neglect this woman inflicted on my children. Looking at her, I felt like I did not know who she was. She seemed extraordinarily ugly to me. I asked Karter if he could play with mommy for a moment so I could use the restroom. Of course, it was a lie. I needed to get out of that room. The anger was back – pushing against me – and I felt the walls closing in. I needed a moment to regroup.

Once in the hallway, I called the CPS worker and explained the situation. She said she would notify the foster home so they could handle it. Back in the room, my ex-wife's family told me they would go get headlice treatment and I thanked them. Back by my son's side, he asked if we could play, as a smile crept across his face. It reminded me so much of that half-smile his brother often shared when he was up to no good. "Sounds like a plan," I responded. "Let's play!"

For the next couple hours, we played with every single toy and game we could – just me and my boy. Neither his mother nor her family ever left the small table where they sat. They stayed there the whole time, talking amongst themselves. It made no difference to me. In fact, it gave me more time with my son, which was exactly what my heart needed. The pure joy and love between us soothed my emotions. We played air hockey and foosball. I let him beat me a few times for good measure. On several occasions, he asked his mother if she wanted to play and each time she responded, "Maybe later." I wondered if this was what his life had been like - always being pushed to the side. After the millionth round of air hockey, I stopped and stepped back. Looking at him, I asked if he was hungry, and of course he was. I asked him what he wanted. It was getting late, and he would have to go back to the foster home soon. I told him he could have whatever he wanted. "CHINESE," he shouted out loudly – a constant favorite of both my boys. We ordered the food and decided it was time to see his brother.

The social worker brought us and Karter into a room first, to go over what he would see and to prepare him for the oncoming assault on his senses.

Thirteen:
A Brother's Last Words

As I PLAYED WITH and visited Karter, my cousin arrived. She sat in the large waiting room while we played. Before our meeting with the social worker, I excused myself briefly and went to see her. After explaining everything I knew, including the results of the first test, I asked her to call everyone back home. I didn't have it in me to make those calls. I also invited her to join us to go and see Kalen. I told her I didn't want to create sides at a time like this, but that it would be nice to have someone with me.

The nurse Rachel picked up an extra shift, so she joined the social worker to talk to us. In the meeting room she had Legos put together, and coloring books spread out. We sat together, with Karter on my lap and his mother seated next to me. The social worker and nurse talked to Karter first, gauging what he knew and preparing him for what he was going to see. They put the little Lego race cars together to give to his brother. They explained everything including the wires, the sounds, the smells, and the tubes. The time had come to go into the room.

As we entered, nothing changed for me. The only difference seemed to be the winter hat on Kalen's head, covering as many of the bandages as it could. A beautiful quilt lay folded at the end of the bed, and he was covered in another beautiful quilt. Tucked in next to him was a stuffed bear. If I hadn't known any differently, I would have thought he was simply sleeping. For a moment, I almost expected him to sit up and greet his brother with that big smile of his. I knew this was just my mind playing tricks on me. I knew that would never happen again.

My son held tightly to my hand, slowly walking inside, and for a moment he was the shadow of a little boy again. He wasn't seven years old, but more like two - sneaking into the room, timid, and scared. We made our way around the room to stand next to the bed. I grabbed Kalen's hand and leaned in to give him a kiss. "Hey buddy, your brother is here," I whispered in his ear, hoping maybe it would bring him life. Karter also leaned over the side of the bed, too short to get close to his brother, and said, "Hi Kalen, it's your brother. I really miss you. I hope you are sleeping okay."

The nurse came around the bed with a stool and leaned in, telling Karter this would help him get closer to his brother if he wanted to. She explained each cord, each tube, and each machine attached to Kalen. She grabbed the stuffed bear from next to my sleeping son. Karter climbed up and leaned his body across the bed. He grabbed his brother's hand, looking back at me for reassurance that this was okay. Of course, it was okay. This was his brother, his other half. For the first time since this began, my two boys were in the same room, and I was struck in that moment at how wrong this was. I was hit right in the soul at how nothing was ever going to be "normal" again, and that my reality and my dreams were gone. The future vanished right in front of me.

I looked at Karter holding his baby brother's hand, and gazing upon him lovingly. In awe and wonder, it transported me back to the very moment they met for the first time. Karter ran into that hospital room so full of excitement. He couldn't wait to meet Kalen, and the love came instantly. I remember Karter telling him that they were going to be best buds, and they were. Now he was saying goodbye to his best friend, and he didn't even realize it. I choked back the tears and moved in closer to my big brave boy. I positioned myself as near as possible to them both. I simply wanted to be in this moment with them.

The nurse brought the bear close to Karter. She said the bear was for him; that it was a magical bear, filled with all his brother's warmth and love. The bear was warm to the touch, having sat on the heated blanket that regulated Kalen's body temperature. Karter grabbed it close. The nurse read the tag tied to the bears' ear. It said, "My name is Mr. Bear, and I am filled with magic. I am full of the hugs and love of your brother. When you hug me, you are hugging him, and because of my magic you can whisper in my ear and your brother will hear you, no matter where you are or the distance."

The tears began to slowly fall from my eyes, as I witnessed this moving gift. Karter grabbed and hugged the bear tighter than I could imagine and whispered into the bears ear, "I love you." The nurse then gave Karter the quilt and explained that this was the blanket they first placed on Kalen when he came to the hospital. She said it was his now, and it would allow him to be close to his brother whenever he wanted. These beautiful gifts would end up meaning more to us than this nurse, or anyone else, could ever imagine. We lingered in the room a bit longer, just sitting - two brothers, holding each other's hands. No one asked any questions.

We felt no rush to move on. We simply experienced it, and for the first time, I could breathe. Then, Karter sat up and as if nothing had happened, and asked if our food had arrived. I broke from my thoughts and looked down, telling him I thought it had. He leaned in, and in the most tender of moments, and the most real of things, just as he had always done, he leaned into his brother. He said, "Hey buddy, we ordered Chinese, so we have to eat now. Don't worry, I'll save you the eggrolls. I know they are your favorite. When you wake up, we can eat them together. So, you have to wake up okay. I love you, bubba, and I will see you when you wake up, and we can play."

My heart shattered in every possible way. These would be the last words Karter would say to his brother, and he had no clue. In his young mind, his brother was going to wake up and everything would go back to normal. How I wanted to be my son in that moment. I wanted his hope; wanted to see life through his eyes. As Karter climbed down from the bed, I burned that image in my mind. It would be the last time I saw my boys together, and I knew it in my being. I wanted it to last a little longer. As we made our way out of the room, Karter looked back and waved to his brother, blew him a kiss, and with a big smile on his face, told him he would see him soon. My heart knew he never would, but I allowed my son his innocence.

Outside of the room, we made our way to the waiting area with the rest of the family, including my ex-wife and her family, and my cousin. During our time with Kalen, my cousin stood silently in the corner of the room while everything happened. She gave me and my son the space we needed in that moment. After we finished, she hung back, and said her own goodbyes. Then she joined us to eat. We sat there laughing and eating, pretending what we just experienced did not exist; that it never happened. As my son ate and visited with his mother and her family, I made my way over to the CPS worker, who sat off to the side watching us and our interactions. I almost forgot she was there.

I took a moment to ask about seeing Karter again the next morning. I gave her my phone number and asked her to give it to the foster family. I said I would like to speak to Karter before bed. In fact, I wanted to speak to him anytime he wanted. She surprised me by saying she already spoke to the foster family. While they never do this, and typically it's against the rules, she gave me the foster family's phone number. She said I could call anytime I wanted. Next, I asked when I could pick Karter up. She looked at me for a moment, then said she wanted to talk to me about that.

The details spilled out in a flurry. She said because my ex-wife remained under investigation – and because we had no other family in South Carolina, among other things – Karter would have to stay in foster care for a while. What did she mean, "among other things," I wondered. So, I asked. She informed me CPS would be formally filing a neglect petition against my ex-wife and her boyfriend. The state would levy formal charges against the man who did this. This made Karter a material witness. They still also had to prove that I was Karter's father. The CPS worker then informed me of a permanency hearing on Monday, at which the court would determine if Karter had to stay in foster care. I needed to be present.

The hurt and anger flared up inside me again. I looked her dead in the eyes and said, "I AM HIS FATHER. I am not under investigation, and I had nothing to do with this." I asked her to give me the details of the hearing, and what I needed to prepare. She said, if you can, bring their birth certificates, your driver's license, and any other documents you want to present to the judge at the hearing. I made it clear, under no uncertain terms, I would be there, and my son would come home with me. I said I expected to see him the following day. She agreed, and I stormed away.

Exasperated, I thought, "What nerve! All these people have some nerve. Don't they care about what happened here? I am their father!" I took a deep, long breath and made my way back to my son, who was finishing up his food. I tucked all the information I just gathered into the back of my mind to process later. I would have to gear myself up for court. I knew what I needed to do, and I would do it, just as soon as I said goodbye to Karter.

We finished up our food, and I told Karter it was time for him to go back to his foster home. He gave me a huge hug and told me he didn't want to leave. I reminded him, this is temporary, and I told him I gave the lady my number. He could call me whenever he wanted, and I would call him before bed tonight. "Go and just be a kid," I said. "I need to be here with your brother." I promised him I would come get him soon, and he would come home. He made me promise repeatedly, then finally gave me a kiss goodbye.

I walked him out and got him into the car, gave him one last kiss, and waved as he drove away. As I turned to re-enter the hospital, I stopped for a moment. I needed to make a quick phone call. I had a friend who was an attorney. I explained everything that was going on. He let me know he was aware of what happened, and he was truly sorry. I explained about the permanency hearing and asked him to coordinate with my dad to get me the needed documents.

In great detail, I outlined the locations of all the documents. After years of court battles with my ex-wife, I had everything in my possession, and organized carefully. He agreed to gather the paperwork for me and fax it all to the hospital, while also overnight mailing them to the courthouse. I gave him the number for the CPS worker and called ahead, granting permission for her to talk to him. Gratitude filled me for this help. He reassured me that no matter what, he would handle everything legal. He told me not to worry. It felt good. I had people in my corner, fighting for me. With that, I steadied myself once again, and went to be with my son.

Fourteen:
Kalen's Last Breath

I MADE MY WAY back inside, through the hospital, and up to the Intensive Care Unit. As I exited the elevator and turned around the corner, I came face-to-face with my ex-wife and her family. Apparently, the doctors had entered my son's room to perform the second test. She let them know I had walked Karter to the car and would return shortly. Moments later, Rachel came out to get us. She pulled me off to the side and said she had made a decision, which her boss approved, and her husband agreed too.

"I am not leaving this hospital until you do," she said. "I want to be with you through it all." This woman became my angel. I spoke the words, "Thank you," and yet they did not accurately express the kind of gratitude I felt in that moment. We entered Kalen's room, hand in hand.

Everything in there remained the same, only this time, a crowd of people and doctors filled the space. "How many people could you fit in here," I wondered. Everyone looked pressed together like sardines in a tin box. I recognized the doctor who ran the first test and some of the nurses, but there were other people I did not know. I saw the social worker and of course, Rachel stood by my side, my hand in hers. Dr. Gomez stepped forward and the room fell strangely silent. The sounds of the machines beeped in the background.

"As you know, we ran the first test this morning, and I advised you that under state law we were required to run the test for a second time," the doctor said. "We just performed that test again. I am sorry to have to tell you this, but there is nothing we can do. For all purposes, under the state, your son is gone. We have not marked time of death, as you will have to make certain decisions. We can no longer administer any medical interventions, as it would be considered mutilation of a corpse under our laws."

He continued, "I am sorry to inform you of this, but you will need to decide to pull the plug or let nature take its course. Now, if you decide to allow the latter, this will be a very slow and painful death for your son. Also, I believe the social worker would like to talk to you and help you with the options before you. Again, I am very sorry."

With that each doctor exited the room one at a time, like soldiers when they begin to transition from formation into single file. This man, with the precision of an executioner, raised his rifle and shot me without a shred of emotion. He remained completely detached and void of empathy. Then, he lowered his gun and left the room. I lost my breath, and a sense of paralysis permeated my body. I could see people walking around me, crying, and uttering words, yet I remained somewhere else, apart from them.

Rachel grabbed ahold of me, and, for the second time, I heard screaming, only to realize the sound came out of me. I was falling fast. Grasping at the side of the bed, I cried out. The most animalistic and guttural noise erupted from a place in my soul. It was as if I stood on the beach, at the precipice of the ocean, watching a tsunami roaring toward me, and I remained paralyzed. I could not outrun it, and no one was coming to save me. I felt the torrent slam down upon me, only this was not ocean water killing me. Pure and absolute grief erupted from some epicenter inside as I experienced the visceral sensation of my soul ripping in half. There I stood, by my son's bedside, fully aware of the violent, churning waters and I was powerless to stop it.

He was gone. My baby was gone. I would not be his father anymore. That realization washed over me in a different way – like the ocean turned to acid. It dissolved everything that made me who I was, leaving bones behind. I had no idea how not to be his dad. I stood there weeping unconsolably until every bit of my humanity emptied out and I lost my breath.

After a moment, I moved into the hallway. I needed to escape my own carnage in that room. I felt Rachel next to me, and I sobbed harder. I looked at her and said, "No one will ever understand. You didn't know him. To you he was just a patient, a little boy who you treated, but he was my son. He loved riding his bike. He loved playing outside and being with his brother. He loved telling jokes."

I couldn't stop. My pitch elevated and my pace quickened. "He wanted to be a cop; and did you know that his favorite movie was Rudolph? We would wake up every morning and sneak into the living room. He would snuggle under a blanket on my lap and watch it with me while he ate."

I was desperate and I unloaded my emotions in the one safe

place I could, with Rachel. "No, you don't know these things because to you he was just a patient."

She held me tighter and let me sob into her arms and whispered something into my ear. "He wasn't just a patient Tim. He was your son, and now I know him better through you. You will help him live on through your memories. He was your son."

She held me and let me sob until I had no tears left inside of me. When the storm finally stopped, she looked me square in the eyes and said, "You are his dad now and forever, and it's time to make decisions only a dad can make. I will be with you until the end." I whispered a thank you and she got to work, caring for Kalen.

I found my ex-wife nearby. The decisions in front of us seemed so enormous. Where do you start, when a storm has pummeled the earth with such ferocity it tore civilization to shreds, leaving apocalyptic destruction in its wake? As we sat and talked, she informed me that, legally, she could not make any decisions on Kalen's behalf, but she wanted to be included. Due to the investigation, the decisions were ultimately mine. I told her we would make them together, regardless. We agreed that pulling the plug was the only option we had. I offered to tell the doctors, but before I could do that, the social worker approached us with another woman.

After the obligatory, "I'm sorry for your loss," and, "I know this is not a good time," the social worker introduced the woman with her. The woman asked if we decided what to do and we said we had. We would let Kalen go peacefully. The woman then asked if we considered organ donation. She acknowledged the awkwardness, but explained, time is of the essence. I could barely believe my ears. Kalen still lay in his bed, not yet officially dead according to the state and the doctors. An image of an old western movie sprung into my mind, where the vultures circle the body, waiting to pick at it. Only, we were the vultures, and the body belonged to my boy. I looked at the two women standing in front of me, and without even thinking, asked them to leave us alone.

A queasiness worked its way up my digestive track and I suddenly felt like I might be sick. Desperate for air, I excused myself and ran as fast as I could from that place. I ran without thinking. I just needed to get the fuck away from it all. It felt like a shop of death from a horror movie. I ran down the stairs to the nearest exit and before I knew it, I stood in that beautiful courtyard again, before the fountain where I imagined Kalen dipping his hand into the water. I worked hard to catch my breath.

I saw the bench nearby and fell onto it. The gravity of everything that happened sat heavy on my shoulders and permeated my entire body, like it weighed a thousand pounds. That weight pushed me down onto the bench and locked my feet on ground as if I were chained there. I sat staring into that fountain as I had once before, envisioning my son playing in it, knowing he never would. I looked up to the sky, which was growing darker, and asked, "What am I supposed to do?"

I cannot explain the feeling of what happened next, but from the top of the buildings surrounding me, as if from heaven, came a butterfly. It floated down through the air and circled the fountain, playing around the mist of the water. It flew directly to me and landed on my leg. A peace settled over me, and I knew this was my son. This was a gift from God – a message of strength. He gave me permission to move forward. I suddenly understood, my son was all things beautiful. After all, what was more beautiful than life itself? My son could give life to others now. I knew what I needed to do and I made my way back inside to face it head-on.

I found my ex-wife and the social worker. "We will donate his organs," I said, without hesitation. My ex-wife looked at me stunned.

"I can't do it," she said. I told her we were, and that we had to. She looked me in the eye for a moment and then shook her head in agreement. The social worker left us and found the lady she had introduced me to moments ago.

The woman came over and reminded us she worked at an organization called Sharing Hope. They facilitated organ donations between families and recipients. She thanked us for making this decision and took us to a room. The woman said we had to decide what organs we felt comfortable donating, and that it was entirely up to us. She read each organ off a list. I felt like I stood at the counter of a butcher shop, choosing the right cuts of meat. I could barely comprehend what we were discussing, as if my son was nothing more than a prize pig, but I pushed through it. After we made our decisions, we signed a litany of forms, and she left us to go tell the nurses. Once Kalen was pronounced dead, they would administer all new medications to allow for the harvesting of his organs. We decided to donate his liver, kidneys, intestines, and heart, among others.

The doctors and nurses learned of our decision and the dreaded time came. We made our way to the room but paused at the precipice. My ex-wife looked at me and said, "I can't do this. He's already gone. I don't need to be present for this." I looked at her in utter amazement, but I would not let my son go through this alone. I entered the room by myself once again, as I had so many times throughout this journey, but this time, something had changed. The atmosphere inside the room felt drastically different. An eerie calm hovered over it. The beep of the heart monitor had a different tone. I stood in the aftermath of the storm.

Rachel worked away, straightening up and arranging an assortment of plungers and syringes full of medication. She explained that she would turn off the machines and disconnect what she needed to. Once they pronounced Kalen dead, she would immediately start the machines up again and administer the medications. They would sustain his heart and organs for harvest. I asked her when we would do this. She said once they received notice they had organ recipients, they would wheel him off to the operating room, but there was no way of knowing the exact time. I looked over at my son once again - too small for the bed he was in. "My small boy. My baby boy," I thought. I noticed on the bed there was a laptop. "What's that?" I asked Rachel.

She walked over to me and said "He was and is your son, always. You are correct, he is my patient, but he is your son. I listened to every memory you shared with me, and I remembered you said that Rudolph was your thing. So, I called my husband while you were meeting with everyone and asked him if he could bring in our copy of the movie. We only live a couple of blocks from here. I explained to him what was going on and why I was working so much. I just couldn't and wouldn't let you go through this alone. I figured you guys could watch it one last time, and you could let me know when you are ready."

This woman, who had only just met us, truly understood me. She had a son Kalen's age, and she was feeling this moment deeply herself. I made my way to the bed, and I whispered, "Thank you." In a quivering voice, I asked Rachel, "Can I, um, get up there with him? Can I hold him?" She looked at me and said "Honey this is your time, don't you worry about any cords or tubes or anything, you do what you want, this is your goodbye. Just tell me when."

I looked at her and I said, "Don't tell me. Just do it when it feels right." I climbed into the oversized bed, scooped my boy up into my arms, and held him. I nestled him into my embrace as if he were a newborn baby, exactly as I had the day I welcomed him into the world. During our first embrace, I feared he was so fragile he might break. This time, however, I feared I would be the one breaking.

"Hey buddy, its daddy," I said. "I know this is hard, and it's okay. You are so brave and so strong, I'm here and it's going to be okay. It's time for you to go home now buddy. Know that I love you so very much. You were always the best parts of me and the best gift I could have ever had." We started the movie and I continued to whisper in his ear. "How about we watch Rudolph, buddy. You remember how we would climb in my chair and watch this together? Of course, you do. You are so brave."

I continued to talk to him as the movie played, describing each scene. I cried as I spoke, but I held back the big tears, because he needed me now. My tears fell and washed over him. "I am so sorry I couldn't protect you, and I hope when you get to heaven you know how much I love you; how sorry I am." Despite my best efforts, I cried harder. When Kalen's favorite song from the movie began to play, I sang along. It was a song of promise for tomorrow, but there would be no more tomorrows for my son. I could hear the pulse of the machine behind me, almost in time with the music. I sang.

"There's always tomorrow for dreams do come true.

Believe in your dreams, come what may.

There's always tomorrow, with so much to do, and so little time in a day."

The machine stopped. Kalen's heart stopped beating and my son died in my arms. I sang on:

"We all pretend the rainbow has an end, and you'll be there, my friend, some day."

On September 16, 2017, at 5:26 pm Kalen passed away as I held him tight. I held him just as I had when he came into this world, and I held him as his spirit left it. I held him as his life played out before my eyes - every laugh, diaper change, and nap in my chair when he was a baby. I saw every birthday, his first steps, him running after his big brother, and flexing his muscles. I saw every tear, bump, and triumph; every hope and dream that he had and that I had for him. It all filtered through my mind – every piece of him left and gone.

I sat there holding him until I heard the machines start back up, knowing that this was no longer Kalen. I held him hoping that if I just held him tight enough, I would wake up from the nightmare. This would all be a dream. I held him until the movie was over, then I laid my son back down and tucked him in as I had done a million times before. I kissed his forehead and hugged Rachel. I thanked her for this beautiful gift she gave me, then I turned and walked out of that room.

FIFTEEN:
NIGHTMARES AND GIFTS

IN THE HALLWAY, I looked for my cousin, my ex-wife, and her family, and I informed them it was done. Kalen was gone. Grabbing my cousin, I wrapped her up in my arms. Then, I told everyone to go and say their goodbyes. Once again, I delegated the task of calling the family to my cousin. I just needed some time. I walked out of the building and allowed the night air to wash over me. Back in my familiar place in the courtyard, I cried. Every single thing in life says that after such a heart wrenching moment, I should have bottomed out. I should have gone back to drinking or became some shell of a human being. I did not do any of those things because, I realized, I was still Kalen's father. Every single second of my life moving forward would be a song for Kalen.

So, I stood in that little courtyard and gave in to the sensations.

An emptiness spread through me. The gravity of the loss grounded me in the present moment, and I allowed myself to feel it without resistance. I could never again be Kalen's father on earth, but I had to keep moving, or the weight of grief would kill me. I reached into my pocket and pulled out my phone. I mustered just enough energy to call my dad, my aunt, my sponsor, and my attorney. My cousin would handle the rest. I announced that my son died and made my way out of the tiny courtyard.

Back in the hospital, my cousin waited in the lobby, wondering where I went. She wrapped me up in a huge hug and quietly said, "I am so proud of you. You are so strong." The fatigue settled in. By that point, I had not slept in over 24 hours, and the exhaustion hit me like a freight train. My cousin said the nurses had papers for me to sign and needed to know if I made arrangements with a funeral home. "Can we do it in the morning," I asked. I also had to meet with the investigators and tell my son Karter the news. I could call the funeral home afterwards. She went and told the nurses for me, and we made our way out.

The hospital made arrangements for us to stay in a house across the street which they used for families in situations like ours, akin to a Ronald McDonald house. I could finally sleep. The hospital staff had been so good to us in our time of need and now, they said we could stay as long as we needed to. I let them know I planned on leaving for New York on the Monday following my court appearance and thanked them for yet another gift.

The house was situated at the back of the hospital, directly across the street. It was a simple Victorian home and remained very non-descript. As we made our way to the door, a very sweet, older woman greeted us. She seemed like she could be anyone's grandmother. The hospital had called ahead and advised her of our arrival. She expressed her condolences for what we had been through and said it was all over the news. I thanked her for her kind words.

She invited us inside and much like the exterior, the house looked undistinguished. If anything, it reminded me of walking into my grandmother's house with that 1950s feeling. Nothing made it look lived-in. The sterile, white walls like inside the hospital itself, made their way into this home. Very few pictures graced the walls. The knickknacks people gather over a lifetime seemed to be missing. It was simply a place to rest and sleep.

Through the living room, we saw a hallway. From the hallway, there were two bedrooms, each with two twin beds and a bathroom. A small eat-in kitchen awaited us in the morning. The woman explained that the home was donated to the hospital and divided into four mini apartments. This was just one of them. She offered me some coffee and explained where we could find a grocery store and other local resources. She would stay and tend to our needs.

I walked down the hallway and into one of the two bedrooms. My mind was spent. I had no energy left to think. Though the woman was kind, I could not talk any longer. I needed to sleep; to escape this nightmarish reality. The room, like the rest of the house, felt sterile. There was no window. The covering and pillow on the bed looked hospital issued. I saw a small dresser and a nightstand with a hospital lamp on top of it. I flopped on the bed, closing out the world around me, or so I hoped, but sleep did not come easily.

The images of the last 24 hours flashed through my brain like a horror show. Each time I closed my eyes, I saw my son in the hospital bed. I saw the bullet wound. Terrifying thoughts occurred to me. What were the last images Kalen saw? Did he feel any pain? I must have slept, though. I only know this because I suddenly woke up to my phone ringing and it said 8:00 am. I had agreed to meet with the investigator at 11:00 but she called to reschedule. We would meet the following day, after my court hearing, and before I left the state.

I hung up, stirred from the bed, and made my way to the kitchen. Finally able to process my surroundings, I noticed a small square table in the corner, much like you would find in a diner. On the counter sat the coffee pot, a dish drainer, and a towel. There were coffee mugs next to the powdered creamer, milk, sugar, and stir sticks. Nothing adorned the walls, not a single decoration. I found myself in yet another sterile room in a stream of them. I grabbed a cup of complimentary coffee and went outside to smoke. As I sat down on the curb in front of the house, I looked up, allowing the newly rising sun to warm my face. I needed to ground myself again, to collect my thoughts, and create a mental list of the tasks in front of me.

I began a Google search of funeral homes and called the first one nearby. I didn't expect anyone to answer. It was too early. So, I left a message explaining my situation and gave my name, number, and the purpose of my call. As I spoke the words, it felt odd to me. Of course, they knew the purpose of my call. Why else would someone call a funeral home? I decided to call the CPS worker next and leave her a message too. I needed to see Karter and tell him his brother died. I still had no idea how I was going to tell my son this news. Just like that, another wave of indescribable pain hit me. My son was gone. He was dead and I would never see him again. I allowed the tears to flow as I looked at the horizon and the rising sun. I felt lost in the moment – lost in time and my own little prison.

When I contained the grief enough to move on, I went inside

and found my cousin in the kitchen where she was eating a muffin. Though I had no appetite, I drank my coffee while she ate. She had been on the phone with my family back home and kept them informed of everything. I found out my father and others sent money for me, and that my dad's friend Jim was on the way to be with us. He would provide transportation so we could get around and then return home after court the following day. My cousin suggested I eat, but hunger alluded me.

I thanked her for everything she had done and promised to call my dad later in the day. I needed to shower and head back to the hospital to sign the paperwork from the night before. Once we were ready, we walked across the street, only this time, the hospital looked less foreboding. It was as if a veil had been removed and I could see it as an ordinary building. People came and went, moving about as if it were just another day. Not a single one of them knew the tragedy that had taken place the night before. I suffered alone as life went on around me. As I looked upon the scene, a profound thought struck me like lightening. Death was a normal, everyday thing here. In this building, death walked the halls in some form or fashion, day in and day out. For its occupants, my loss was routine – nothing unusual or out of place. It was all in a day's work. They treated patients and guided families. While each person who experienced loss in these walls arrived as a stranger, they left behind remnants of their existence like flakes inside the concrete itself. When they moved on, their essence hovered here forever.

When I entered this time, I would not go the way I had before. I entered through a private door and made my way to the place where my son had been – where his body still was. I walked to the double doors and pressed the call button. A voice came over the speaker. "How can I help you," it said. I had no answer to that deeper question. "This is Timothy Sherlock, and I am here to sign some paperwork," I responded. The voice on the other end responded, "Please wait a moment," and then the double door swung open.

Standing there, on the other side, was Rachel. This beautiful angel waited for me – my rock in the raging sea. She was the one person who had been my moor through the entire journey. My worry and sadness lifted for a moment, and a sense of calm replaced it. "I'm going to be okay," I thought. I had Rachel. "What are you still doing here," I asked. "I told you I would be here until the end," she said.

As we walked, Rachel explained that my ex-wife was still at the hospital, in the room with our son. Apparently, she refused to leave until they took him in for the surgery to harvest his organs. It struck me as odd. I wondered why she seemingly acted on maternal instincts now, after not being present when Kalen passed away. I decided not to think about it. I had a task to complete.

We made our way around to the center of the ICU and approached the nurses' station. My eyes caught a glimpse of the room where my son's body awaited its next steps. I saw my ex-wife sitting there with her mother and made my way with Rachel to sign my name on the papers. I just wanted to escape this place. I could feel the anxiety building inside me again. As we neared the desk, Rachel, handed me a stack of papers. They included authorizations to harvest the organs, liability forms, and last but not least, the death certificate.

This final piece of paper stunned me. This wasn't a high school diploma or a trophy from little league. This piece of paper certified something I never imagined would happen. When I held the tip of the pen to the line, I certified the death of Kalen. I made it official, and I hated that. Of course, Kalen was dead. I held him while his heart stopped beating and the machines went silent. Yet, there it was. A single piece of paper declared the truth as if it were a living thing itself – the final, cold period at the end of a sentence.

This made Kalen's passing far too real. Tears ran down my face as I swept the pen across the page, leaving behind my ink-stained name as if I held this awful truth alone; as if I were the only human being on earth who could tell the world he existed. As a father, I had to confirm my son was gone and our earthly relationship gone with it. Rachel asked if I made arrangements with a funeral home yet. The hospital had to arrange transport, which required my authorization. I told her I called a place, but had not settled on a decision yet. She said to call her when I had the details, and they would fill in the blanks. I signed the paper.

As I turned to leave, Rachel stopped me. "Tim, wait," she said, "I have something I want to give you, if that's okay." I felt stunned by that statement alone. Hadn't this woman given me enough already? She stood by my side through the worst tragedy of my entire life. She never left, not for a moment. What more could she possibly offer? She hurried to the other side of the desk and came back carrying an arm full of items. "I cannot imagine the loss you feel," she said, "but I wanted you to have these things." She handed me a canvas upon which spelled the world "Love." Kalen's handprint graced the surface. I could touch the very spot his hand had laid. In red, replacing the letter "O," they spelled out his name, date of birth, and date of death.

Next, Rachel handed me the quilt that covered him when he passed away, and a red blood tube with a piece of paper inside it. She explained that the piece of paper contained a printed recording of his last heart beats. Finally, she handed me his socks. Though policy typically dictated against such a practice, Rachel and the hospital wanted me to have as much of my son as they could give me. His little socks, which touched his skin, felt like an actual part of him. The tears ran down my face in streams. This woman would never know how powerful these items would become to me.

I set the items down on the nurses' station and wrapped Rachel in an embrace as tightly as I possibly could. In time, I would come to understand that so many moments on this journey surpassed language. Any parent who has lost a child this way would understand. Human vocabulary cannot accurately contain these experiences. Looking at this beautiful woman and the gifts she presented proved one of those moments.

When our embrace came to an end, I turned and saw my ex-wife and mother-in-law. Once again, I walked slowly into that room. In a mechanical way, I recounted my plans to them. "I left messages with a couple of funeral homes, and I signed all the paperwork," I said. "Are you aware of the permanency hearing scheduled tomorrow?" I explained I would go to the CPS office that afternoon to see Karter, and tell him his brother died. She asked me to call her when I scheduled a time so she could be there. "More than likely, I won't come back here," I said. I had no need to return to the hospital now. "When will they take his body in for surgery," she asked. I reiterated what the staff told me. They would move Kalen's body when they had organ recipients. We made small talk and I left.

My cousin and I worked our way back across the street to the sterile little house where we found a lady cleaning and straightening up. She looked up and acknowledged us, then went back to work. You could see in her eyes she knew who I was, and she knew what had happened. How odd to be recognized for this – for the death of my son. After a moment of contemplation, she stood up.

"I am so sorry to hear about your son," she said. "It's in all of the papers and on the news." This time, the words took me by surprise. It almost felt like an invasion. The news of the shooting and Kalen's death, broadcast for the world to hear, put our heartbreak on display. This wasn't some soundbite, some sensational story to boost ratings. This was my son, my life.

All the same, I witnessed something familiar – people hurting deeply over Kalen's death. That shared grief – even as it paled in comparison to my own – meant something. I thanked her for her kind words, and I meant it. "There is some paperwork in the kitchen for you, that the hospital sent over," she said. We made our way inside. As I began to open the package on the counter, my cousin brewed coffee. Inside the envelope, I found copies of all the paperwork I asked my attorney friend from New York to send to me. This marked the next process I would face – another courtroom where officials would decide what to do with Karter. I took a long sip of my coffee and readied myself again, but this time, I faced another battle, and this was a fight I was familiar with. From the moment of my divorce, I existed in flashes of courtrooms, pleading time and again for my sons. Only this time, I was fighting for one son instead of two. This time, I would win.

As I hustled around the house getting ready for the day, I felt my body and mind switch over to autopilot. Thank God for my cousin, keeping me on track, and giving me small tasks to take on. Without them, my mind might have disappeared into the foggy waters. I could see it, off in the distance, looming in. It wanted me – to scoop me up like an empty vessel and pull me out to sea. I had no bearings, no idea where to find my north. So, the tasks kept the fog at bay. I made a few phone calls and set a time to see Karter. I spoke with the funeral director and scheduled an appointment for the next morning before court. I talked with the attorney in New York and with my family. Amid all this, my father's friend arrived. He booked us a hotel room with the money my father sent, to get us into a new space for the night. We packed up our things, bought some fresh clothes, and went to face the day. Our first stop: to see my son Karter.

SIXTEEN:
A GAME OF BATTLESHIP

THE OFFICE FOR CHILDREN and family services sat inside a smaller building in the heart of downtown, in a run-down area. We pulled up to the building as my ex-wife and her family arrived behind us. We spilled out of the vehicles and greeted one another. My ex-mother-in-law told me her husband was on the way. He had arrived in South Carolina the previous day. I felt lifted by this. Karter – in fact, both my boys – loved their maternal grandfather. It would mean a lot to Karter to see him.

My ex-wife looked at me as we stood there, and said she wasn't sure what to say or do. "Does anyone?" I thought. Even with all my training as a therapist, no handbook existed on how to tell a child their brother just died. I looked at her and said, "We'll just go with it, and God will do the rest." We talked a little bit about the court date the next day, and I told them I had an appointment with a local funeral home. I asked if they wanted to come with me, and in a similar fashion since I arrived, she decided she couldn't possibly handle any of it. She left me to make all the decisions. When the CPS worker arrived, she showed us into the building. Karter would arrive soon after. We entered a small playroom where they provided supervised visitations for families. It looked nothing like the game room at the hospital where I met with Karter earlier, but there were toys and board games sprawled about. I rummaged through the shelves and found the game Battleship. I had spent countless hours over the summer playing it with Kalen and Karter before bedtime. They loved it.

With a plan in mind, I turned to the CPS worker. "They had to cut Karter's hair," she explained, to prepare me for when he arrived. "Why," I asked. Apparently, the volume of lice he had required it. Then she added something. "They also needed to conduct follicle samples as part of the police investigation." I felt so confused. Why would they need follicle samples from my son, I wondered aloud. The worker indicated my question might be better suited for the police. I took this piece of information and filed it away in my mind, knowing I would talk with the investigators later. I shared that detail with no one and sat waiting for Karter to arrive. I began to run through the words in my head – words I knew would devastate him.

My cousin sat beside me, and we began to chat. Looking at her, it felt nice not to be alone, to have someone safe there with me. It felt like I had been plunged into a raging war. It was no secret that there was no love lost between me and my ex-wife. Our divorce had been brutal, and each subsequent court appearance felt equally horrible. I believed, in that moment, she was the reason we were all here in the first place; the reason I was about to tell my oldest son that his baby brother died. Once again, as had happened so many times before, that hot, piercing rage filled me up and I pushed it back down. This was not the time or place. Expressing my anger could come later. For now, I had to be a dad.

Karter arrived and burst through the doors. I scooped him up in my arms. Gosh, I needed this. I needed to feel something real. As I hugged him and placed my hands on his arms I knew, this was how it was supposed to be. I pulled him in and squeezed him tight, with all the love I could give. I hoped my own tenderness would permeate his body and he would know just how much he meant to me. A bottomless well of emotions rose through me, and I felt the tears rising to the surface. I pushed them down. I needed this. My soul needed to hold him. I kissed and kissed him, like I did when he was little, eliciting that childish laugh from deep within him.

"DEE DEE STOP," he squealed. I set him back down, and he said hello to his mother and grandmother, giving them both quiet little hugs. It struck me, the difference in our relationship with our son. Karter and I were always so close, loving, and affectionate. When it came to his mother, it felt somewhat disconnected – cold and formal. I noticed how he stood apart from her. The love existed there, but it was more respectful, more closed. That real closeness seemed to be missing, as if it were a "supposed-to-be" love, like a code of etiquette.

Karter had no hair on his head. It shocked me, as I looked at his skin with barely any stubble. We wanted him to feel confident, so we commented on his cool new "do," and his slick new look. "I like it," he said. He recounted how hot it gets in South Carolina. "Now, when I go outside to play, I won't sweat!" He was certainly making the best of an awful situation. He and I made our way over the table where I had the game of Battleship setup. "Do you want to play," I asked him. A light flashed in his eyes with pure excitement. He knew what this meant. "Only if you're ready to get your booty beat," he said. "Oh, you think do you," I retorted, "You're on." Battleship was a competition in our house to see who could out-think the other person and reign as champion. I always arranged my ships in the exact same configuration, ensuring it was easier for him to win. I think he knew this, but he always played as if he had no idea where my ships were.

We played the game, talked about his hair, and how things were going at his foster home. He said he loved it there. He talked about jumping up and down on the trampoline and asked if we could get one. They had chickens and he would chase them around. "There's one chicken that lets me carry her," he said with glee. "There are a lot of kids to play with and they are all really nice," he told me. He had his own bed to sleep in, but, with an air of seriousness, said he didn't like sleeping alone. "Sometimes, the lady lays down to help me sleep."

We simply sat talking, father and son, playing a game as if nothing happened. I lived for moments like these, but no matter how much fun we had, the cloud of Kalen's death hung over our heads - a storm cloud which threatened never to move or pass. It was oppressive and suffocating. I looked up at my ex-wife and her mother and signaled for them to come over. They walked to the table and sat on either side of Karter. "Who is winning," they asked. Of course, he was. "Hey, buddy, Mommy and Dee Dee have to talk to you." Lord, I didn't know how to do this, but I powered on.

"Sure thing, after I win this game," he exclaimed, as the unease settled onto his face, almost as if he knew what was coming. "No bud, I need you to pay attention." He looked up from his game.

"You know how Kalen got hurt right?" I asked. "Yeah Dee Dee, but it's okay, the doctors are going to fix him. That's what they do, right?" He asked this question while looking me dead in my eyes.

"Well buddy, doctors do fix boo boos, but sometimes there are boo boos that they just can't fix." How was I going to say this? I could feel my throat closing as I looked at my son's face. How was I supposed to destroy this little boy's hope? Why did I have to be the one to do this? It isn't right, I thought, and it isn't fair, but what other choice do I have? I continued, "And well, they couldn't fix your brother's boo boos buddy. Do you get what I am saying?" He looked down at the game and asked me softly, "So Kalen isn't going to wake up?"

"No bud, he isn't. Kalen died buddy. He went to heaven. But I want you to know, he isn't in any pain, and that mommy and daddy love you so much and that we are here buddy." I could feel the tears welling in my eyes, waiting for my son to break down. He never did. He looked at me, and in a flash, I saw the realization pass through his eyes. I saw a split second of devastation, then just as quickly, it disappeared.

"Dad can we just play Battleship?" he asked. It was the only thing my son said to me. I realized that this was all too much for him to process. Hell, it was too much for even my adult brain to process let alone his. "Yea buddy, let's play Battleship." I would not push him any further. I would allow my son to work through this in his own way, and I would be there to be his dad through it all. We sat there at the table and continued to play Battleship, pushing all the terrible things away. For a moment, sadness did not exist. We moved the hurt aside in place of love, laughter, and joy together. I allowed myself to be present with those gifts – to lose myself in the game with my son.

Some may call it a trauma response, and it is, but I felt grateful. Our bodies and minds knew exactly how to protect us – to give us the space and time it would take to heal. Or, perhaps God knew. I looked at my son and remembered what it was like when he was a baby, when I first became a dad. I thought of the promise I made, to protect him always. I remembered every single reason I wanted to be a dad; and I realized I still was one. I was his dad. Sure, the hurt remained and in the recesses of my brain I knew the pain would come rushing back to devour me – but not now. Not in this moment. This moment was for me and Karter. This moment was a gift from God.

Eventually, the woman from CPS came over, and very calmy told us it was time to wrap things up. I didn't want our time to end. Didn't she realize how important this was? It seemed so unfair. I needed time with my son. We needed time together, to face this as one. It felt so unnatural to send him back off to foster care or to have someone tell me how long I could see him. Suddenly, all the anger of the last few years culminated inside me - all the missed opportunities when my ex-wife wouldn't let me see my kids. Now, one of them lost their life, and this worker represented all of it. I told Karter to go sit with his mom. I walked up to the woman and begged her for more time. My heart lay bare in front of her. "We just told Karter his brother died," I pleaded. "I need to know that he's okay; that nothing bad is going to happen to him." I thought of some of the twisted stories I heard about foster care throughout my career and I winced with fear.

"He should be coming home with me. None of this is right," I declared. She simply agreed. This woman had no power over the decision. In fact, she said she was doing everything she could to get Karter back to me, and I believed her. In court the next day, she promised to recommend Karter be released into my custody, but her bosses were pushing back. We talked a little while longer and then the time came. I walked over to Karter to tell him it was time to go. "I promise I will see you tomorrow," I said. He looked intensely sad but put on a brave face. He did not cry. He simply said, "Okay," and gave me a huge hug. "Will you call me before bed," he asked. "Of course, I will," I assured him. "Don't you worry buddy. I'm going to bring you home."

After the visit we went to eat, but I still felt no hunger. It went beyond a lack of appetite – not like when you go to a restaurant and none of the options appeal to you. I wanted the nothingness. It felt like a choice my brain needed to make. As I sat at the table, I looked off into the distance, completely numb. Not a single thought entered my mind. My body simply existed there. During lunch my phone rang. I answered and the gentleman from the funeral home spoke. While he had a busy schedule the next day, he could see me now. "Hell, why not," I thought. "Let's just add more shit to the pile. What does it matter." They finished up their food and off we went.

On the way to the funeral home a brand-new set of questions alarmed my exhausted mind. When would his body be released? How long before we heard from the organ transplant team? Could there even be an open casket? No, his head wounds were far too gruesome for that. The litany of pounding thoughts halted when we arrived. Sure, I had been to funeral homes before. I dealt with death in my life, but death and these arrangements made no logical sense. This funeral home looked like any other funeral home I had entered before, but never on this end of things. As I walked from the car to the door, a deep desire overcame me to honor my son in the best way I could. A man in a suit greeted me and escorted me to a tiny room. It probably served as a dining room in some other place and time, where families gathered for a meal and enjoyed conversation and laughter. A large table sat in the center of the room, with dozens of binders spread across it, no doubt the limitless options to be presented to me.

The man, whom I categorized in my mind as a generic prototype of a person, started with the typical sentiments. "I'm very sorry for your loss," he recited. "Have you given any thought to what you want done?" After that, the questions flew from his mouth like a flock of birds. This was his job and it was second nature to him. He recited a memorized script, completely oblivious to me. What type of casket do you want? Will there be a viewing? Will you do this back in New York? Where will your son be buried? Who will get his body, you or your ex-wife? Would there be any conflict over this? Depending on who gets the body, how will you visit the burial site? Will you take turns?

I withstood the assault of questions and responded simply, "The best possible decision is cremation." I told this caricature in front of me that I wanted the ashes divided in half so that one set of ashes could go to me, and the other to his mother and her family. They could do what they wanted with it. From there, we discussed the price, and I paid half the amount immediately. My ex-wife and her family remained responsible for the other half. The man accepted the arrangements but warned, "I will not release the ashes until the total bill is paid." I assured the man, the bill would be paid, thanked him for his time, and walked out. What did it even matter at this point? Kalen was dead and never coming back.

I spent the rest of the day gravitating in and out of a fog-like state full of distant memories. I felt like I was sleep-walking. Every now and then, I talked on the telephone, into the vast expanse of a parallel universe. "How is mom doing with her chemo," I asked my father, or I listened to a concerned friend recount words of care and support. Through it all, I continued to exist on that plane of nothingness where I had no emotional or spiritual energy whatsoever. I did make sure to call Karter before bed and I got all my papers ready for court. I climbed underneath the covers and tried to sleep the best I could.

SEVENTEEN:
HELD HOSTAGE

T HE NEXT MORNING, I woke up in the hotel room my dad's friend booked for us, to the warm sun shining on my face through the window. Its brilliance made my skin hot. I felt suspended somewhere in between that place of consciousness and slumber. When the sun pulled me from my deep sleep, a slow swirl of thoughts, images, and senses surrounded me. It seemed like a strange cacophony of hopes, dreams, reality, and existence. My mind attempted to regulate the moment; to make sense of where I was and what was happening. I wanted to stay sleeping, tucked away in the warmth, safety, and comfort of the blankets. I wanted to stay right there and never feel pain again, to alter my reality. The last thing I wanted to do as I lay in that bed, the residue of sleep still evaporating away, was to think, feel, or make decisions.

The mental fog slowly lifted and as it dissipated, my senses kicked into high gear, grounding me back into the world. Whether to God or just to my own spirit, I prayed for strength for the day. All I wanted to do was take my son and go back to New York; to lay my other son to rest and get on with my life. I wanted to leave this nightmare behind me and never come back to this place again.

I sat up in bed, feeling old for the first time in my life. Everything hurt and felt heavy, as if I were moving through pudding, or like my entire body was wrapped in ace bandages, constricting, and prohibiting me from being youthful and swift. In my mind I went through the check list of things I needed to do. I had to prepare mentally for every possible outcome. I had to meet with the investigators and wondered what kind of questions they had for me, or what information they might give this time. Their words could never bring peace or closure. My son was gone.

I also had to go to court. I had all the documents proving me to be Karter's father. What could possibly go wrong, I wondered. Legally, he should be with me. I could keep him safe. The night before, I talked with my cousin about the possibility of Karter and I staying with her family back in New York. After all, I had just packed up my apartment to move to South Carolina and gave up my lease. Essentially, I was homeless again. This thought suddenly sent me into a spiral, and that familiar and awful thing happened. My mind was overtaken by fears and questions.

How could I be in this position? Would my landlord be understanding given the circumstances? How would I get all my stuff out of the apartment? Could I really raise my son on my own when I could barely function right now myself? A panic attack slammed into my body like a ghost train veering off the track, and I couldn't breathe. My heart started racing and my palms turned clammy with dewy sweat. I rushed to the shower, allowing the hot water to run across my body and ease my mind. I needed routine now. The shower and the thought of a routine grounded me and held the panic attack at bay. I felt steady again. The waves of despair that were beating against my body, the way a turbulent sea pounds the sand, receded.

I needed to get my shit together, that much I knew. In the deepest recesses of my being, I believed God had a plan, and I could do this, simply because I had to. As I started to get ready, I realized I had no clothes appropriate for court. Why would I? I had no reason to think about that when I sped off from New York to be with my dying son. So, I dressed in my normal clothes like a normal man in a not so normal situation. I made my way to the breakfast area to find my cousin and my father's friend.

"Honey, they have eggs, bacon, yogurt, toast… you really should eat something," she said. "You haven't eaten in two days." I could sense the motherly concern in my cousin's voice, but I just wasn't hungry. I smiled at her, and thanked her, but opted for a cup of coffee and a cigarette on the patio. Was this my new norm? They followed me outside and we sat in the sun, they with their food and me with my coffee. My father's friend said he would drive us to the courthouse, and from what he could tell by MapQuest, it was about 20 minutes away. Then he would take me to meet with the investigators. My cousin asked if I wanted her to come with me or if I wanted to do this alone. I had already done so much alone in the last two days. No, I wanted her there.

The courthouse was a perfectly square building that rose high up. People milled about in all directions, coming, and going. It looked like a fortress, foreboding and looming, just daring me to breach its surface. A pit settled in my stomach. I knew what to expect, honestly. From my days working for Child Protective Services back in New York, and my time as a litigant in my own family court matters, I knew. I spent years of my life fighting with my ex-wife and pleading with judges. "Here we go again," I thought. Then, I remembered the judge in New York - the one who called me dramatic when I said one of my sons could die. If only that stupid judge had listened to me, we wouldn't be here now. If only I had never used drugs; never gave them a reason to mistrust me. If only... If only...

I knew standing there beating myself up and reliving the past couldn't help with what lay inside that fortress of a courthouse, so I took a deep breath and entered the building. We stood in line waiting to go through the metal detectors and watched as our belongings moved slowly down the belt to be scanned and processed. I always found it off-putting how each person coming into a court building got assessed based on their perceived threat level. They pre-judged us on our appearance, even before we stood in front of a judge in a court of law. I often wondered why this process felt so uncomfortable. Wasn't the law supposed to be blind; to be fair? Standing in that line to be scanned and checked, it all seemed incredibly unfair.

We made our way up to the floor where our proceeding would take place, when a guard suddenly informed me that we could not enter the court. Apparently, there was a dress code. Could he be serious, I thought, incredulously. "Excuse me," I demanded. "Are you really serious right now?" I said it in the most disdainful voice I could muster. I truly meant this man no disrespect, but after all I had been through, someone was really going to worry about how I was dressed?

"I am sorry, sir, but sneakers are not allowed in the court room. I don't make the rules." His thick southern accent spoke politely but issued a warning. I responded fast. "Sir, in the last 48 hours, I found out my son was shot, and my other son was being held in foster care. Then, I sat and held my son as he died in my arms. Only then did I find out about this court date. I am not from this state, nor do I care about some arbitrary, STUPID rule about sneakers!" I was shouting at this point, and became aware people were stopping and staring at me.

"Now, I don't know who you have to call, or what you have to do, but I am going into that courtroom, and I am going to get my son even if that means you have to arrest me. Am I making myself clear?" I could not tell you where that came from, but this poor man just suffered all my hurt and anger, bottled up over these past few days. We stood staring at each other, almost willing the other one to move. You could cut the tension with a knife. Just then, another guard made his way over. He whispered something into the man's ear. After their brief exchange, he stepped away and made a phone call. I could feel the glare of everyone in the vicinity settling squarely on me. "I apologize sir, you can go through," he said. "But just be prepared the judge may not be happy." I could not believe my ears. The judge may not be happy? What the hell did I care if some judge was disappointed in my shoe choice in his or her courtroom. Before I could dig myself into a deeper hole, my cousin pushed me along and thanked the officer. She hurried me to the elevator.

"You are going to have to keep it together," she told me firmly. "You cannot act like that. I know you are hurt and angry, but Karter needs you and you have to pull it together." She was right, and I took another deep breath in the long line of deep breaths I had been taking for days. My son needed me, and I needed to conduct myself in a decent manner. We exited that elevator and checked in with yet another officer. Then, we made our way over to a small waiting area. A sea of people bombarded my senses. Among them, I saw my ex-wife and her family. The CPS worker stood off to the side. When she spotted me approaching, she made her way over and said, "We're up next." The moment was drawing near.

I asked if she knew what was going to happen in there. I needed some sense of what to expect; some kind of preparation. She said, "I don't know," and handed me back all the documents I'd already provided to her, to her supervisor, and to the attorney. I muttered out a thank you and began pacing around the room, completely unable to sit still. I moved and moved to avoid the crushing anxiety swelling up inside of me. Around and around, I walked through what seemed to be a million people; but there weren't a million of them. Just the same ones I kept passing, over and over. Then a voice boomed out and called my case.

Everyone under the umbrella of "Karter Sherlock" moved through the doors. The courtroom did not resemble what you see in movies, in any way at all. Nor did it look like the courtrooms of New York I'd grown accustomed to back home. This looked like a pop-up venue, thrown together in a flash for a sudden event. It had a traditional bench for the judge. Two tables sat facing the bench, assumingly for the defense and the prosecution. Folding chairs sprawled out in the back for everyone else. We settled into our designated seats with me at one of the tables. The judge began reading the petition into the record. Once complete, she asked to hear from Child Protective Services regarding the allegations in the case. Essentially this outlined all the things that transpired, leading to Karter's placement in foster care and the need for this court appearance.

The attorney representing CPS told the judge Karter's mother was under investigation, and they thought it prudent for Karter to remain in foster care until a family member or a permanent placement could be found. Addressing the attorney, the judge said she was under the impression that the father was in the courtroom, and she wondered what was prohibiting me from having my son. It seemed more sensible, she said, that he be with his father rather than in foster care given all that happened. She looked at me and asked if I was Karter's father. I stated I was indeed his father, and that I supplied the court and attorney with copies of my driver's license, birth certificate, social security card, and the birth certificates of both my children. What happened next, I never saw coming.

"Your honor, we did receive the paperwork," the attorney for CPS said, "but we have not had time to assess if this gentleman is truly the father or not. The documents are photocopies. Further, no case worker has been able to assess his home for safety, and to truly determine if being with him would be in the child's best interest. As the child has resided in the State of South Carolina, he falls under our jurisdiction. There is a process, as you know, your honor."

The words hit me like a freight train. I felt stunned. "Your honor, if I may?" I asked. The judge motioned for me to speak. "Your honor, the argument that counsel makes is at the very best a reach. My son has identified me as his father, as noted by the caseworker that has been supervising each visit. I have supplied each and every document necessary, proving I am who I say I am, and I am the father. I find it rather ludicrous that a complete stranger would fly down here, sit through the death of a child, meet with investigators, and be given the authority to make life and death decisions over a child, including donating his organs, if that person wasn't the father of the child. Does this attorney mean to say that his own caseworker, the police department, and the hospital personnel are all wrong in determining me as the father? My son has been through more than any child should EVER endure in such a short lifetime. I have endured more than any parent should ever endure. Common decency, and common sense, would dictate that my child and I be reunited and allowed to grieve and move on. Keeping him in foster care serves no purpose but to further his anguish."

I stood there staring at the judge, hoping that my words spoke to her, and that they were enough. The judge looked out over the room, pondering. "Sir, I have looked over your documents," she said, "and although you make very compelling points, and I am very sorry for what you have been through, all of you, the law is clear." She continued, "The Department must complete its investigation, and its due diligence, to ensure the child's safety, and as such the child will remain in their custody until such time it is deemed otherwise."

I broke. "Are you serious," I responded, "and what am I supposed to do? How long will that take, and what about my son?" I started yelling.

"Sir, that is enough," she said in a very stern voice. "I would suggest you get an attorney, and if you cannot afford one, you may go and file for a free attorney, but that is my ruling sir." I did not care.

"This is absolutely ridiculous," I shouted. "I cannot come back and forth to this state while you hold my son hostage and do whatever it is you are going to do. You are punishing my son and me for something that neither of us had anything to do with. I am not the one being investigated." Before I could finish, the judge yelled over me, hitting her gavel hard on the wood. Once again, she said, "Enough," and threatened me with contempt of court. I saved her the trouble. In the middle of her sentence, I walked out, pushing my way through people, the judge still yelling in the background. I just didn't care at that point.

Out in the hallway, my cousin came right up behind me, followed by a blond-haired older woman. She introduced herself as the court's victim advocate. She took me to a room to fill out papers for a court-appointed attorney, which I did not intend on using, and I left the building. Outside I sucked in a deep breath along with the the intense heat of the sun. My mind raced wildly, anger and adrenaline coursing through my veins. There was nothing I could do right now. The decision was made. I would have to find another way to be with my son. My life from the moment I arrived in this God-awful place was a series of jumping from one problem to another to another. I had to constantly direct my focus to the next big thing. I suppose it helped me survive. I could not slow down. I could not take a moment, so I simply accepted it.

Before leaving the courthouse, I spoke with the CPS worker and made arrangements to see Karter before leaving town. I told her I still needed to meet with the investigators, and then I would see him. I called my friend who had been handling the legal things back in New York and broke down for him what happened in court. Immediately, he said he would file in New York, and to let him know as soon as I was in town. We would meet and come up with a plan. I looked at my cousin and told her there were a couple of things I wanted to do before we left for home, if that was okay with her. She agreed.

EIGHTEEN:
THE CRIME SCENE

WE LEFT THE COURTHOUSE And made our way to my first stop. Despite my cousin's objections, we drove to the crime scene; to the place my children called home. I needed to see it and to know where it happened. I wanted to see where they played. We drove down twisting dirt roads, past cotton fields and horse paddocks, until we reached one very long and sandy dirt road. I felt immediately struck by how desolate it was. Surely this could not be the right place. My ex-wife was a teacher and I felt certain she made decent money. Why live all the way out here, I wondered. We made it to a small, white trailer that looked no bigger than a camper. It was beat up and run down. It sat in the center of a sun scorched, sandy yard, slightly faded. A small wooden deck that served as the porch was positioned in the center of the trailer. It had no railings, and the wood was sun bleached and split.

A Song for Kalen

Looking at the windows, I could see sheets and blankets hanging in place of curtains. For all accounts, I could not see my sons living like this. When we divorced my ex got the home. My boys had a huge two-level house, each with their own bedrooms. Everything was newly remodeled, and it sat on two acres of land. What would bring someone to leave all that behind to live a life like this, I wondered. I made my way through the sandy yard to sit on the small porch. Kids toys littered the yard, and a small children's pool sat off to the side. Remnants of play could be seen everywhere. The pool had glow sticks and toys in it. Bikes lay outside. I knew I couldn't go inside because this was a crime scene, so I sat on the tiny porch looking at the yard. I saw the imagined years pass by like a film, creating an image of what it must have been like for my boys there. I imagined my sons swimming and splashing in the water; dunking their heads underneath to escape the hot southern sun. I pictured them running through the yard and jumping in the little pool. Perhaps Kalen just sat in it, playing with his action heroes as if they were real.

I could hear their laughter in my mind. Then my thoughts jumped forward and I imagined Kalen riding his bike in lazy circles. He would look back and yell, "Dee Dee, look, no training wheels! Look at me go!" His big smile spread across his face and for a moment, the image felt so vivid, I thought I could reach out and hug him. I could not, and the images faded fast, like ghosts of another life, hunting me with their weapon of illusion.

The truth crashed down on me once again, ripping the beautiful images away. "He'll never ride his bike again," I thought. I turned my head and looked over my shoulder at the worn and battered door. My heart became sick. On the other side lay the home my children ate in. In there, they watched television, played, and slept.

On the other side of that door mayhem occurred. On the other side of that door my son lay in his bed. He had kissed his mother and brother and told everyone goodnight. He had probably read a story and tucked himself under his blankets as he always had, not knowing that when he drifted off to sleep, he would never wake up again.

On the other side of that door, while he slept, he would get shot and die. The anger rose in me like bile trying to erupt from my stomach. I stood and ran to that door; I kicked it and punched it with everything I had in me. I screamed and beat on that door with my bare hands, wanting to rip every piece of this tin can apart. I wanted to eliminate every detail that ever existed of this house of horrors. I kicked and punched and clawed and screamed, until there was nothing left, and I crumbled to the deck, sobbing. I sobbed for the life my children had led. I sobbed for the life that Kalen would never lead, and I sobbed for the life Karter would have to lead without his brother. I sobbed for myself too: for the choices I had made, for the reasons they were down here in the first place. I sobbed out of sadness, grief, and guilt. I could not protect my children. I could not protect my son and now he was gone and never coming back.

I would never get to say I am sorry as he listened, and I would never hug him and hold him again. As I started to calm down, I took a few deep breaths. My chest moved deeply with each one. Exhausted from whatever just happened, I sat there for a moment looking out over the yard. A horse farm sat on the other side, with what I was assuming to be an electric fence, separating the horses from this yard. The horses stood and looked at me. Their tails flicked back and forth. Their ears twitched to keep the flies at bay. They looked at me and I could see they somehow felt my pain. I envisioned my kids looking at these horses and loving every second of it. I made my way off the porch, tracing my path back to the car where my cousin waited, wondering what I must have looked like a moment ago, and feeling thankful that she gave me the space to have that breakdown.

As I made my way back through the yard, I paid closer attention to the piles of toys that lay scattered around. In one pile, I saw his tyrannosaurus rex. I got it for him over the summer. He insisted on bringing it home because it was, after all, the king of dinosaurs. He had spent hours playing with it at my house. In fact, he even insisted on sleeping with it. How could a simple piece of plastic bring a child so much joy; I would never know. A smile flashed across my face at the memory of buying it and of my son carrying it around everywhere. I picked up the toy and carried it back to the truck – a memory I could grasp, a piece of him. I knew it didn't make sense at all, but memories were all I would ever have, and this toy was my son.

It served as a concrete memory of the boy that once existed. I walked slowly back to the truck, feeling old and tired, and even more drained, if that were possible. I looked at the passengers in the vehicle looking back at me – my cousin and my father's friend. Grief, pain, and loss painted their faces. There would be no words, I knew this. What words could there be? I had no other choice but to push on, to methodically check the items off my to do list. This was my existence: one task to the next. This was my reality. It was how I functioned. I wondered, would I ever go back, or would I always be this way?

NINETEEN: CODE ANGEL

MY NEXT TASK WAS one I didn't think I would do. Earlier, I had told my ex-wife I would not be returning to the hospital, but now I had to. Before seeing the investigators or taking on any other tasks, I wanted to thank the staff at the hospital. More importantly, I hoped Rachel would be there. She never knew how much her love and support meant to me. I stopped and bought a couple trays of cookies and sweets, and I made my way to the hospital. Once back in the ICU, a look of shock crossed Rachel's face when she saw me coming. The ICU was much the same and offered a sense of comfort to me, weirdly enough. I had just spent so much time here, it felt familiar. I made my way to the nurses' station and set the treats on the desk. I asked her if she ever took a day off and we laughed.

I gave Rachel the biggest hug I could and thanked her repeatedly for all she had done. I was so grateful for all she had given to me and to my son in his final moments. As we chatted, I could sense something was different with her. I asked her if she was okay. Then, Rachel told me something. This was going to be big; I could tell. She said that every nurse has "their one," and for her, Kalen was the one. She could no longer work in the Pediatric Intensive Care Unit. The situation proved too emotionally difficult. I completely understood. I always wondered how someone like a nurse could do that sort of job day in and day out. As I stood there thanking her for all she did, a soft and sweet voice came over the loudspeaker. They announced a "code angel" and asked all available personnel to report. The message repeated several times. I looked at her puzzled and asked if she needed to go, as I saw people making their way to the hallway.

A smile spread across her face, and she said, "Come here, I want you to see something." She took me by the hand and led me to the hallway. What could she possibly want to show me now? As we made our way to the hall, I could see it quickly filling up. People were lining either side: doctors, nurses, custodians. An array of colored scrubs, business suits, and various uniforms dotted the walls. They painted either side of the hallway in a rainbow mosaic.

"What are they doing?" I asked Rachel. "What's going on?"

"When someone passes, and they donate their organs, they are seen as an angel, granting life to another through their death. We honor that, and honor that person for their unselfish gift." She directed me around the corner. "Now we honor your son. This is something special and unique. This has been all over the news and in the papers. This community has been devastated by this. We do not have children like Kalen here often. Your son's tragedy has affected this community, and this hospital very deeply. The gift you have given through his tragedy should be honored." Her words hung on me in that moment. Time slowed, and everything seemed surreal. The words tragedy, gift, unique... They stung me, but also planted something more beautiful deep inside of me. I had not thought of anything that had happened as unique or a gift. However, in this moment, it was a gift. I could see my son's life coming full circle. I was witnessing the impact that his small existence had on a community and would have in other communities. He would impact so many families with the organs that were being donated.

As I looked in the direction she pointed, I could see a bed being wheeled around the corner. In it, lay the body of my son, still hooked up to the machines. I knew this wasn't my son. My son had been pronounced dead already, yet there he was, his chest moving as if he were breathing, his heart pumping blood to the rest of his body. This was all artificial, I knew, but for a brief moment I hoped again that as they wheeled him down the hallway he would show some sign of life, that he would wake up. I knew that he was gone, and that he served a larger purpose now, and perhaps always had. I too would honor my son in this moment. He was finally a hero. As they walked his bed down the hall, each person stood tall and saluted my son. Tears streamed from some of their eyes. Others had their hands over their hearts, but every person honored the life that once was. They blew a kiss or nodded their heads as he passed. This was not just a few people. It was hundreds. I walked with my son to the elevator, and down a few floors. When the doors opened another line of people waited. Every staff member in the hospital, it seemed, lined those halls. They honored and memorialized my son's life all the way to the operating room.

These were complete strangers. I knew as I watched the incredible scene unfold before me, his death was not for nothing. It would bring new life to another human being. No greater gift could ever be given. My son could leave no better legacy behind. I too received a gift in that moment – a gift I'm not sure I deserved. It gave me reassurance that, as a father, I made the right decision. When the "code angel" finally came to an end, the time also came for me to go. I stopped at the double doors that read, Authorized Personal Only, and watched as my son's body disappeared down that hallway, on to the next stage of the process. The doors closed slowly as he disappeared from site.

This time, my heart did not shatter as I thought it would. This time, a sigh of relief came out, and a sense of pride filled me. My mind danced around, imaging what the people would look like that would get his organs. How old were they, what did they have going on, and how long had they been waiting for a miracle? I then wondered how their families would rejoice and cry at the fact that their loved one would get an organ, that they would be saved. Then I wondered if these same families and people realized the grief a father was feeling because his child, his loved one, had to die to save theirs. I turned, and again, hugged Rachel. I thanked her for yet another beautiful gift. She would never know the impact it would have. I turned slowly and made my way back to the entrance to the hospital. I passed the same doorway that lead to the chapel where I had fought with God, and passed the door that lead to the small courtyard where I had encountered the butterfly. I walked out the double doors and back into the sunlight. I made my way down the sidewalk to the parking garage where my cousin awaited, looking over my shoulder at the hospital that had cared for my son, and cared for so many others. This was no longer a place of death, but a place of hope. I knew that. I also knew that my journey wasn't done. I still had much work to do. I needed to make my way to the investigator's office.

TWENTY:
CHARGED

BACK IN THE CAR again, we made our way to the next stop. I mentally recounted what had just happened in the hospital, while looking out the window at the landscape flashing by. I could not fully grasp what I just witnessed. As I tried to understand that moment in the hospital, I looked out at the colors, fields, and flashes of scenery. My cousin and the man driving sat quietly as I recounted the many faces I saw as we walked through the corridors in honor of my son. As people in those hallways cried, I realized they too knew the amazing gift presented in that moment. The profoundness of it sat with me as we continued our journey.

It wasn't a terribly long drive to the investigator's office, maybe 20 minutes or so. The State Police Barracks, where the investigators' offices were housed, were situated in the middle of nowhere.

A concrete and brick building seemed to literally appear out of thin air in the middle of a desolate field, encased by a sea of black-top and parking places. A few police cruisers painted the parking lot, and a large shield emblem adorned the door we parked closest too. If not for these talismans, I would have thought we were in the wrong place. My cousin asked if I wanted her to come with me. I thanked her, but as I had done during other moments of the process, I knew I needed to do this part alone.

I entered through the emblemed door. In front of me, I saw a receptionist area and a small waiting space with very little seating. No one sat at the desk. A short woman came walking up to me from somewhere off to my right. "Mr. Sherlock?" I looked confused as I stared at the woman. Was I supposed to know her? "Please call me Tim, my father is Mr. Sherlock. Do I know you?" I asked, as I reached out my hand.

She took it and introduced herself as Ms. Valentine. We shook hands and she asked if I had time to sit and talk with her, to go over things. I let her know I had family waiting in the car, but that I had as much time as she needed. I only planned on meeting my son around 2:00 p.m. and then, head back to New York. She escorted me through a doorway and through an office area. There were several small cubicles in this room, and some people sat in them, talking on the phone. I assumed they were other investigators at work. We made our way around the workstations to what appeared to be a conference room. The room was exactly what you would imagine in a movie: old wood paneling, metallic blinds covering the window, rows of very old filing cabinets along the wall, and in the center, a metal table with four metal chairs.

I made my way to one of the chairs and the investigator sat perpendicular to me. She had a notebook and a folder in her hands.

She placed them on the table and apologized again for everything I had endured and said that she only had a few questions for me. "How well did you know the person who shot your son?" She asked me. What a strange question I thought, it wasn't like we were friends, or having family dinners on Sunday. I lived in New York, and they lived here in South Carolina.

"To be honest, I didn't know him all that well at all. I had met him only a couple of times when he brought the kids to New York to visit me with my ex. Other than that, I only know what my kids told me. He was kind and good to my kids," I responded. "My ex left and moved down here a couple years ago without me knowing. It's a very long story. I had planned on moving down here in a few weeks myself."

She looked at me, making a few notes in her notebook. We sat quietly for a second, though in that moment, a second felt much longer. She went on, "Sir, there are a lot of moving parts to this case, and not all the details are known yet. I know you probably have a lot of questions, and sadly there is very little I can tell you at this time." I looked her in the eyes and allowed her to continue. The meeting only lasted a short while, mainly because they gave me most of the information already. I knew my ex-wife's boyfriend confessed, but since Kalen died from the injury, they were charging him with negligent homicide. I also learned they were charging my ex-wife with criminal facilitation and negligent homicide. Both would be charged with criminal neglect of Kalen and Karter.

It felt frustrating. I wanted to know how everything happened, and why. Sadly, they could give no answers. They had not yet formally filed the charges; therefore, the investigation was considered pending. My mind swirled around this news about my ex-wife. "Are you sure she had a part in this? Was she responsible for this?"

I asked. The investigator looked me directly in the eyes and said, "There is no doubt in my mind, or anyone else's, that your ex-wife was responsible for this as much as her boyfriend was. Trust us when we say this was no accident. I cannot give you the details, but I would start making formal requests for the paperwork, and I would ask for the coroner's report."

I could barely process this new information, and it merely led to more unknowns. So, I tucked it away. The investigator then made an assurance: my ex-wife and her boyfriend would not get away with this; Kalen would have justice. That last word struck me as funny. "Justice?" I thought, "Kalen would have justice?" There was no justice in a situation like this. A gaping wound tore open inside me the day that bullet struck my son, and now part of my soul was missing. There would be no justice – no closure – because there never could be.

Before leaving, I shook her hand and thanked her for the information. She told me she would keep me informed at every step, and as soon as formal charges were made, she would call me. She said I would hear from the State Attorney to discuss the next steps. She then gave me the information for the coroner and told me how to file a request for information. If they were allowed to release them, I could try and get the coroner's report and the police files. I thanked her again and shook her hand as she opened the door for me. I stepped into the Southern sun. It suddenly seemed so much hotter. It was now mid-afternoon, and I had about a half hour drive to go see Karter. I made my way across the parking lot to the truck where my cousin and father's friend waited. I wasn't sure what I wanted to tell them; this meeting really had offered nothing more than I already knew. The only difference now is that I knew what the charges would be, and I was leaving with more questions than I had before coming.

As I got into the truck, I relayed the very little I had been told to my other companions as we made our way back through the countryside. I still could not get over how rural everything was here – just miles and miles of fields and farms. As I relayed the information to them, I was struck by how many things kept changing quickly in the course of my time in South Carolina. I wasn't sure how I could keep up this pace, but I knew that there was so much to do still. I could see no end in sight. Perhaps this was my existence, a living hell of keeping busy and trying to stay one step ahead of the crashing grief that threatened to swallow me at any moment. Visions of my son played in my mind yet again. I had thoughts and saw images of his last moments, followed by images of him as he was before the gunshot. It was just too much to sort through or tackle. I pushed the thoughts out of my head and closed my eyes. I shut out the world and focused on my breathing, knowing that I was going to see Karter, that I was going to hug and hold him. That would steady me, for now.

Twenty-One:
A Father's Wrath

On the route to see my son, the countryside gave way to urban areas. I thought of it as the concrete jungle of the south, if you will. The roads became more even, and fields turned into sidewalks and neighborhoods, then faded into buildings, and people, and traffic. We made our way back to that decrepit, rundown building where I would visit with Karter. It looked artificial, drab, and ominous. Maybe it was just my emotions painting the picture before me, but this building offered nothing of promise. It appeared to be a place where children were taken away from families. It seemed to house abuse, neglect, fear, and sorrow. At least, that's how I perceived it.

Walking inside felt very different this time. The day before, I had hope. I believed I had a real shot at taking my son home with me.

As we sat playing Battleship less than 24 hours ago, I gave him the worst possible news: your brother died. I recalled that flash of trauma and devastation in his eyes, and how it recoiled just as quickly as it arrived. His brain, like my own, did what it needed to do to cope with the worst possible thing. To make it better, likely for both of us, I made him a promise. I said I would be back to get him. Now I had to walk back inside and deliver more bad news. I had to tell Karter he couldn't come home with me. This time, I had no hope as I entered through those doors. That judge and that court proceeding stripped away any opportunity for this moment to be a happy, joyous reunion.

Not to mention, how much devastating news should one child endure? How many times would I be made responsible for delivering heartbreak upon my son? It suddenly felt like every bad choice and decision I ever made in my life was catching up with me, as if this were my punishment for not being present sooner. I knew – and would be reminded – that this was not true, but despair has a way of trapping us inside our darkest weaknesses.

When I walked in, the CPS worker greeted me. She let me know Karter would arrive in 15 or 20 minutes. They were running late. She also told me that their director would like to talk to me. I was not expecting this and could not imagine what this person would want to talk to me about. Given the department's stance at the hearing earlier that morning, accusing me of not being the father of my own child, and doing all they could to keep me from my son, I was pretty sure there was nothing to discuss. All the same I agreed to meet with him, and stated that my cousin would be joining me. Given the amount of anger I felt inside at that moment, I knew it was not wise for me to meet with this gentleman alone.

She showed us to a doorway, where a short, middle aged man stood waiting. His grey hair was slicked back and parted, and he wore a blue dress shirt with a matching tie and a pair of dark dress pants. He reached out his hand and introduced himself, extending his deepest regrets. He showed us to the two seats situated in front of the large oak executive desk and made his way around to sit on the other side. Clearly this wasn't going to be an informal how do you do. We sat in silence for a few moments until I decided to break the ice.

"Can I ask what exactly it is you want to meet with me for?" I tried my best to keep my voice level and even, trying to conceal the disdain I felt for this man, for no other reason than he was the head of this department keeping my son in foster care and away from me. He folded his hands in front of him and leaned in, "Mr. Sherlock, I wanted to take a moment and extend my deepest sympathies. I know that today's court appearance greatly upset you. I want you to know that we take the care and protection of children very seriously, and only have the best interest of your son and his safety at heart. There is a process here, through the inter-state compact. When it comes to providing proper documentation, the process must be adhered to, especially when releasing children from foster care and looking at permanency..." Before he could say another word, I placed my hand up in front of myself, signaling him to stop talking.

"I am going to stop you right there sir. Let me inform you of a few things. I am no stranger to how this process works. Perhaps you are not aware; I worked for the Department of Child Protective Services in New York State many years ago. I have sat on that very side of the isle in court, so I am all to familiar with what is and isn't supposed to happen. I know how long the inter-state compact and these types of matters can take. I have no intention of waiting that long to bring my son home, nor do I have any intention of sitting here and listening to you pander to me or my cousin in an attempt to make yourself feel better about what you have done here. What I am going to do is go and see my son. Then I am going to head back to New York and work on getting my son home. In the meantime, let me make this very clear to you. I am watching you - every move you make, every decision you make, and the exact treatment of my son. I have already lost one child, and I will not lose another either literally, or to a corrupt system. Let's be honest, having him in foster care makes you money. If there is one hair out of place, one new bruise, if he calls me and says that he isn't being treated right, I will come down on this agency with every bit of power I have and the entire wrath of a father mourning. Am I clear!"

I must have stood up while yelling at him, because I noticed I was already standing and could feel my cousin's hand on my shoulder. I could feel myself breathing very heavily and felt the rage burning behind my cheeks and my eyes. The gentleman sat, leaning back in his chair, attempting to put more space between himself and me. The only barrier that remained was the big executive desk. He looked at me, and in the most timid of voices, so quietly I almost didn't hear him, he said, "Mr. Sherlock I am very aware, and promise I will do everything. I have a grandson who is five and I could not imagine losing him. I am so sorry."

Before he could utter another word, I turned. I offered no goodbye and no handshake. I offered nothing at all. I simply walked out of the room and made my way back to the front lobby. I did not have time for this. I was here to see my son, and that was going to be my only focus. Once in the lobby I took a few deep breaths, and looked out the window. With perfect timing, I saw a van pull up and my son jumped out. My boy was here. I pushed my anger away, put a smile on my face, and made my way to the door to greet him.

TWENTY-TWO:
I'LL BE BACK

I STOOD BY THE glass doors waiting, and I watched as Karter got out of the car. He wore a pair of basketball shorts, and his tan colored Rosemont Zoo t-shirt he had gotten that summer during his time with his grandparents. His shaved head reflected the late afternoon sun, while the rest of him glowed with that beautiful oaken color that he got when he tanned. Standing, waiting to cross the parking lot, he spotted me. The largest most radiant smile spread across his face, just as it always had when I would see him. Every visit, every time he came, that smile appeared. I was transported back to a simpler time when it was just me and my kids, having fun and feeling the love. As he made his way across the parking lot, I came out and ran to meet him halfway, scooping him up in my arms. A joyful "Dee Dee" erupted from his lips with a laugh. He smelled of soap, and a little sweat. His skin was soft, but his hug was immense. I held tight to him, walking back to the building. I wanted him always to be in my arms. I set him back down when we reached the sidewalk in front of the doors. He grabbed my hand, and looked up at me, "I knew you were coming back Dee Dee, I knew it! When do we get to go home?" He looked up at me as he asked the question, hope filling his eyes. "Soon buddy, but how about we visit and play some Battleship? I still need to beat you," I replied. How was I going to break his heart and tell him he would not be coming home with me?

We set up the game and began playing. After a little while, I explained to him what the courts had decided. He would have to stay here for a little while longer. Once again, his eyes told me the story. He was heartbroken, but my brave boy said he understood. He asked me how long he would have to wait; how long he would have to live with this new family. I had no words for him. I honestly had no answer. How long would the courts keep my son there? The only thing I could do, was to promise him that I would be back in two weeks, no matter what. Then I reminded Karter, that is not your new family. You have a family. I told him, "I am your daddy, and I am going to bring you home."

I hated this. I hated leaving him there with strangers. At the same time, in my heart, I somehow knew he would be safe and okay. This time I made another promise, an easier one to keep. I said I would call him every single day and I would not stop fighting until I brought him home. Finally, the time came to go. Karter and I shared one last hug. I picked him up and held him tight. He began to cry, for the first time since this all started. As he cried, I met his tears with my own. I held him close and tight and reassured him that I loved him. I told him I needed him to be brave, and that this wasn't goodbye, but rather, "Until next time." With that, he made his way back toward the van. Walking out the glass doors, he looked at me over his shoulder. My heart shattered a million different ways. I wanted with every bit of my being to run outside and grab him, to throw him in the truck, and simply drive away. Instead, I waved and blew him a kiss as he drove off. I knew I would see him again.

I walked outside, exhausted and defeated, and climbed back into the vehicle. That was it. The time had come to drive out of this state and leave all of this horribleness behind for now. I had so much to do. The drive would propel me through my grief because I had a goal and a direction now. I would never stop until Karter returned safely to my home. While it devastated me to leave him behind, it did give me the opportunity to focus. Back in New York, things would not slow down. I needed to set up a new home, move my stuff, meet with my attorney friend, go to court, and plan Kalen's funeral.

Because I chose cremation, there was no need to wait to have the funeral. It could take place right away, using photos of my son in place of a casket. I had no desire to drag this out. It did mean Karter wouldn't be there, but in my heart, that felt like the right decision. He was seven years old and given everything, I couldn't see him facing a funeral. He should not have to confront all the people and their reactions. The hardest part about leaving Karter honestly came from another place inside me. I did not want to be alone. I always hated leaving my sons. Back in South Carolina, I said goodbye to one son forever. I could hardly bare to say goodbye to the other. I wanted him near me, beside me, with me. It's honestly all I ever wanted. Not having that before led me to a horrible rock bottom and a downward spiral into addiction. I needed to take care of myself, and unlike before, I knew that sometime, some way, my son was coming home.

TWENTY-THREE:
LIFE IN FAST FORWARD

BY THE TIME THE car hit the highway, weaving its way from South Carolina to New York, my body crashed. It could not keep up the pace I'd endured for one second longer. I fell asleep and I slept almost that entire drive up the East Coast. We drove from Hartsville, South Carolina through North Carolina, Virginia, West Virginia, Maryland, and Pennsylvania. Without stops, that drive is about 11 and a half hours. I can't say how long it took us. Completely drained, I desperately needed a break from the brutal cycle of anguish, anxiety, decision making, questioning, and dissociation that became the norm over the last few days. I needed to escape into the nothingness of sleep where the emptiness, pain, and loss couldn't reach me. I woke only a few times to use the rest room when we stopped for gas, and once to eat.

I made a few phone calls to family and to my dad. My mom was weak, and the chemo was taking a lot out of her. She had gotten sick again and was currently in the hospital. My poor father was dealing with all that I had been through, the loss of his grandson, and taking care of my mother 24/7. I explained to him that I would be living with my cousin for the time being, as she had the room, and I had not renewed my apartment. I told him I had reached out to my friends in recovery and that one friend had rented a U-Haul, and that they were all meeting me Tuesday morning, as soon as I got back. We would move everything to my cousin's house. I tried to focus on nothing more during the drive than what was next, and what I could think about in the moment. The heaviness of my life pressed against me from all sides, but I knew I was leaving that all behind. I left that anger and sadness in the South. I had a job to do, a mission, and I needed to prepare a life for my son as I laid another to rest.

We arrived at my cousin's home in Portville, New York, around 2:00 p.m. the following day. It was sunny, and her home sat back in the woods. It was beautiful and more than anything, it felt peaceful. I had called my friends that were helping me move and they were already at the house awaiting my arrival. I felt astounded by the love and support my community showed me. The connectedness was refreshing, unlike the isolation I felt in South Carolina. Here I was able to pass off my responsibilities and delegate things to others, unlike the past few days. Down South, it was all on me. I didn't have to make all the decisions, and I felt joy beyond measure not being alone. In a single day, we moved all my belongings from my former apartment into my cousin's garage except for my bed and clothing. Those, I moved into her spare room. Because I had already packed all my belongings, the move was rather easy. The entire move took no more than three hours, and we were back and finished in time for dinner.

As much as I wanted to be alone at times, I felt comforted being surrounded by family. They seemed to hone right in on my needs. They kept their distance when and where I needed them to, and when I couldn't tolerate the aloneness, they surrounded me. In addition to moving, on my first day home, I invited my friend the attorney to dinner. He had filed an emergency petition on my behalf and the turnaround was fast. We were due in court the very next day. There really was no rest for the wicked, I thought. He informed me that, since the judge wanted to hear my case so quickly, it looked very promising. It was nice to have this moment. The table was filled with family and friends, laughter, and normalcy. Life did go on and would go on regardless of what loomed over our heads. With papers filed and a court date set, we turned our attention to the funeral. I handed a major part of the planning over to my family. They could bring me in on things that needed approval, but I wanted them to do the bulk of the planning. I needed to delegate. I needed to divide my focus, and I knew I could not do it all on my own.

My family and friends asked questions about what I wanted then went about making it happen. The service would be on a Saturday. My brother prepared the obituary and I reviewed it, adding a few touches I felt were important, so that people could understand my son and the loss we just endured. Then, we submitted it to the newspaper. My father took care of the church and the flowers. My family went through all the pictures they had. I gave them my photos as well, so they could create poster boards for people to view at the service and remember my sweet son. The only real request I made was for the brunch. In the brunch following the funeral,

I wanted them to serve peanut butter and jelly sandwiches made with grape jelly – Kalen's favorite.

To my surprise, my cousins started a Go Fund Me page while I was in South Carolina, and I was astonished at the amount of money they raised in a short period of time. Boy, did I need that. I wasn't working because I was about to move, and could use that now for things like moving expenses and setting up my own place eventually. The busyness that began in South Carolina carried over into New York and when I wasn't doing something, I found myself lost in thought, my mind wandering aimlessly. I did not think about anything specifically. It was a numb sort of lost. Here and there I worked on my son's eulogy, trying to find the right words to honor his life and what he meant to me. What's better, every single night and every single morning I talked to Karter. We kept it simple. We talked about his day and the fun he was having. We would talk about the fun things we wanted to do in New York, at my cousin's house. I worked hard to temper my emotions around these conversations, trying not get my hopes up too much. I knew having the courts in New York intervene was a long shot. I was living moment to moment. I could not get caught up on what could be, thinking about Karter and the courts, but I could not live in the past either. I had to temper my expectations of the future with had happened and the reality in front of me. "It is what it is," I thought, and I forced myself to simply exist in the present moment.

Twenty-Four:
Jurisdiction

W EDNESDAY CAME. THIS WAS ground zero: court day. I awoke
to the autumn sun breaking through the blinds in my room. I
must have slept, and it looked late. Since returning home, I had
no memory of ever falling asleep and could recall no dreams. I
simply closed my eyes and then opened them again. Perhaps my
brain was as empty as my soul felt. I rolled over, and strained to
hear if anyone else was up. I looked at my phone and saw it was
7:00 a.m. The kids were already off to school, which meant the
house was quiet. I laid there for a moment, trying to play out all
the possibilities that could happen at court, and the likelihood the
judge would rule in my favor. I was not optimistic, but I knew that
I would fight harder than I ever had. The thought of going back to
the same courthouse where only two years prior the judge ruled
to allow my ex-wife to remain in South Carolina, against all my

pleadings and warnings that this very thing could happen, enraged me, and made me sick to my stomach. I took a deep breath. I could not and would not go to that place of anger. I needed to remain positive for my sons. I made my way from the bedroom, grabbed a cup of coffee, and headed out to the back deck where my aunt and my cousin already sat talking.

I sat down next to them at the small patio table, looking out at the woods. It was a truly beautiful and peaceful place. As I sipped on my coffee, we made small talk. I listened to them chat about their plans for the day, and gazed into the woods. Karter would love it here, I thought. There were plenty of woods to explore and hike, a rope swing to play on, and kids to be entertained by. As I gazed, I could see him running through the woods and laughing, with his brother close at his heels. This is the life they should have been living - running, playing, and being innocent. My heart ached, wishing they could be together. With all my heart, I wanted to see them run around again, but I knew I would never have that.

There would be no more tag and frolicky chases. They would never laugh together again or share secrets with each other. The grief hit me like a tidal wave, all at once, and it crashed hard against my heart. I sat there and cried, pretending what I saw before me was real and not just an illusion created by my mind. I sat there watching them play, and weaving memories into the scene as if it were reality for a while. I knew a scene like this could never exist again, but for that moment, I allowed my mind to create its own reality. Slowly the images faded, and I made my way back into the present moment. The tears subsided. I told myself I would at least make this a reality for Karter. I would give him the life he truly deserved. I finished my coffee and went to take a shower and dress for court. The shower was hot and relaxing, and I allowed it to wash away all the sadness and stress. I pulled out my dress clothes, making sure this time, unlike in South Carolina, I was well dressed and not wearing sneakers. I laughed to myself at the thought of it, as I laced up my dress shoes.

I picked my attorney friend up at the house and as we drove, he explained how he thought the day would go. He showed me two photos of my kids, which he took off my social media and blew up on poster board. He wanted the judge to look at the photos of the kids to remind him of why we were there. I liked this idea. I wanted the judge to put faces to the names he was making decisions about. I wanted him to see who his decision would be impacting. I arrived at court early with my friend, and honestly, did not expect much. This pattern of existence and my disappointment in the court system left me empty inside. I also believed we would be going in front of the very same judge from before. Part of me hoped he suffered; that he felt he played a part in my son's death. In a strange turn of events, the courts decided another judge would hear our case.

It appeared that a Family Court judge in another county had swapped places with this judge for a period of time. Newly elected, he could not preside over cases he once prosecuted as County Attorney. Maybe God was on my side after all. I knew this new judge. He was fair, smart, and compassionate. I prayed for the kind of turn of events my heart and spirit needed. I hated being at this courthouse, hated being back in this place. I hadn't been in this court since the judge ruled that my ex could keep my children in South Carolina. That very decision had led me right back here yet again.

We made our way into the courtroom, and we were the first case the judge would hear. The courtroom seemed cavernous. I looked up at the enormous, tall ceilings, the large oak desk with the witness box, and the two parge tables for litigants. I felt so small in the room. Once everyone was in place, my attorney went first. He made a passionate argument to the judge, pointing out that the boys never should have been removed from the state, and that New York State, because of this, still had jurisdiction over Karter. As such, the judge had the authority to release him back to my care. After reviewing all the paperwork and hearing the arguments, the judge spoke. For so many days since that very first call my ex-wife's mother made to tell me there had been an accident, the bad news piled up like a mountain of anguish. Now, it was as if I climbed that mountain and stood at the precipice.

Despite the trauma, the busyness, the swarm of emotions, and the fatigue, I hiked to the top of that hill and stood. Would I stand victorious this time? The judges' next words washed over me like baptismal water, rejuvenating me, and rinsing all the hurt and torture of the last few days away. The judge ordered that Karter be returned to me. He even went as far as calling the judge in South Carolina directly, while in the courtroom, and he ordered my son to be released to me the following Monday. He cited that South Carolina never actually had jurisdiction, because the mother violated a Supreme Court order by removing my boys from the State of New York in the first place. He also awarded me temporary, sole custody and placement of my son. Tears ran down my face, as the judge set another date to provide my ex-wife the opportunity to be served and heard. I thanked him repeatedly. He had no idea the immense weight his decision lifted from my body, my spirit, and my mind.

As we exited the courthouse, I hugged my friend and thanked him many times over. We made our way to my car, and I could hardly contain my excitement. I called my family to let them know the good news. As we made our way back to my cousin's home, I made a flurry of phone calls. I called my ex-wife and her family. I shared the news from court and gave them all the details about the funeral. I knew they remained down south but wanted them to be invited. They could attend if they wanted to. It felt like the right thing to do. I told them I would be down to get Karter after the funeral, and would set up times with them when I knew more.

My next call would be to my son. My spirit soared like a hawk floating in the sky above the treetops. I could not wait to hear his voice and to tell him I would be there Monday. He was finally coming home. I kept my promise. Karter got on the telephone and like usual, he told me about all the fun he was having. He said he was sleeping well, and that mommy, Grandma, and Grandpa visited him often. After he finished, I paused for a moment and said "Duder, the judge said you can come home! Dee Dee is coming to get you on Monday! You get to come home Duder!"

He yelled with excitement. In a flurry, I could hear him telling his foster mother over and over and over again. "My dad is coming to get me! He is coming to get me!" After he settled down, she took the phone from him, and I relayed everything that transpired in court. I said I would call the CPS worker and update her as well, and that yes, Karter was coming home. She told me that was wonderful news before giving the phone back to my son. Karter asked if it would be okay for him to bring his things from his mom's house and I told him he could bring anything he wanted.

TWENTY-FIVE:
BREAKING POINT

 THE REST OF THE week back home in New York flew by like a
jet plane. I went to a flurry of meetings for my recovery program –
usually at least once a day. My sponsor came with me and having
that person nearby meant everything to me. They had lost their
daughter two years before, and they deeply understood what I was
going through. To say I didn't think about using would be a lie. I
thought about it almost daily, and through many moments of the
day. I wanted nothing more than to not exist at times, but I would
think of my beautiful son coming home, and think about all that I
had overcome, and I would know the drugs were not a solution to
my problems this time.

People came and went from my cousin's house, dropping off
food or offering comforting words. Others just came to check in

on me. I wasn't eating much, but it was soothing to know people cared about us. I would have a bite of this or a sip of that, but I really lived off coffee and cigarettes. Having people constantly showing up or calling kept my mind from slipping into the darkness of despair. I felt like I needed to show people I was doing okay, so the phrase "fake it until you make it" became my motto. As I approved the funeral arrangements for Kalen, I realized I needed to go clothes shopping, which proved to be a much greater challenge than I expected.

One afternoon, I made my way to a store in town which housed a nice men's clothing department. As I made my way to the men's section, I wondered, "What does one wear to their son's funeral?" I stood back, looking at the selection of black dress shirts, black pants, and ties of many colors. With each new pair of pants or shirt I looked at, I felt myself sinking down further and further into a sea of black. Suddenly, it was all I could see. Everything turned black, like a swirling, nauseating darkness churning in on me. "I'm buying clothes for my son's funeral," I heard in my mind. The darkness went deeper and deeper until it closed in on me. Suddenly, I felt a hand on my shoulder and heard a voice ask, "Are you okay?" I found myself sitting on the floor in the middle of the store sobbing. I had no idea how I got there, and I snapped.

"Am I alright? No, I am not all right!" I said back to the stranger. "I am buying clothes so I can go bury my son! No, I am not fucking alright!" I yelled. I stood up, grabbed whatever I had in my hands, and made my way promptly toward the checkout and the exit. I paid for my things and left. Once outside, it took great effort to steady myself. I could not believe I had just done that. I was both embarrassed and saddened that I behaved that way. I was also shocked at where it came from. I made my way back to the car I had driven there and collected my thoughts. I needed to not dwell on this. I felt like what I needed, was to stuff it back into a place in my brain where I could lock it away. I needed to focus on other things, anything. I looked at my list of things to do and called the school to get the ball rolling for Karter's enrollment.

I visited my mother who was back in the hospital with complications from her chemotherapy treatments. Not much was said, other than a how are you, and a hug and kiss. This was particularly heart breaking. My mother was my best friend and I had not been to see her, nor had I talked to her since I had returned. I didn't know what to say to her, and I just could not face breaking her heart or causing her more pain than she was already in. My dad would relay messages and keep me informed as to how she was doing. This time she had fluid in her lungs, and they were pretty sure she had pneumonia. I told my father I just needed to get through all this, and then I would be there to help him care for my mother. I felt so guilty asking my father to help me with so much, knowing he already had so much on his plate.

Through it all, I just needed to keep busy; to maintain a routine, but there were moments of silence. During my down times I allowed my mind to wander and to let the grief flow through me. It did not yet feel like the watery flow of a healing grief. It felt painful and acidic and physical. Sometimes, I thought I might actually die from it. Sometimes, I begged God to let me die. Staying busy was better. Little did I know that in addition to my grief, I was traumatized. All of these moments and these reactions were trauma-based. It would take me years to sort through all of that.

Amid the trauma, sometimes, I would see Kalen out of the corner of my eye, as if he were still alive. I would see him playing in a room or running through the trees in the woods out back. At night, while I slept, I heard his voice yelling for me, asking for help. I would wake up, startled and alert, and search the house only to realize he wasn't there. I could not protect him. I did not know at the time I was suffering from symptoms of post-traumatic stress. I felt I was doing just fine all things considered. I truly was not.

For my cousin and her family, for all intents and purposes, life went on as usual. Sure, she had just walked me through this moment, and I was living at her house, but she got her kids up and ready for school every day. They shared laughter, arguments, and family dinners. It seemed so unfair in contrast to what my Kalen suffered; to what Karter and I suffered. Yet, as much as it hurt to watch them, it also brought me joy. It elicited beautiful memories for me of my own kids and gave me hope for the future. I learned lessons about life and so much more.

During that time, I sat for hours, writing, and rewriting my son's eulogy. I just could not find the right words. How do you capture someone's entire spirit, soul, and lifetime in a collection of letters? How would I even get through it? Every day as I sat staring at the page, I prayed for peace, wisdom, and words. I began to retrace moments. I thought of all the memories that made up my son's life on earth, yet every time the pen met the paper, I got lost. "A father is not supposed to do this," I thought. I was supposed to go first. I did know one thing. My son was all things pure, and all things love. He was laughter and light. I thought of his crazy outfits and how he danced around the house. I thought of him playing outdoors with his brother, fishing, and camping. Every minute of his life ran through my mind on an endless loop, encoding his essence into my very DNA. He was my hero, my angel. As I gave into the memories that spilled over me, the words formed. An image emerged in my mind of the portrait of my son. I knew exactly what to say.

TWENTY-SIX:
A FUNERAL FOR KALEN

"TAP, TAP, TAP," I heard next to my head. I slowly opened my eyes, still blurry with sleep. "Tap, tap, tap," again, coming from the window next to the bed. I drew back the curtain, to find a small bird tapping at the glass. Apparently, it was time for me to get up. The day had arrived. I flopped myself back down into the bed, drew the covers over my head, and exhaled deeply. I did not want today to happen. If I just stayed where I was, then maybe it wouldn't happen. Logically and rationally, I knew I had to get up and get moving, but I just wasn't ready. "How many times do I have to say goodbye to my son," I wondered. Then a thought struck me. Today isn't about me. Today is about every life Kalen touched. It is about honoring that and giving his impact its moment. Today wasn't a goodbye, but a celebration of a life remembered. It's amazing how a single change in perspective can shift an entire psyche. My body relaxed. Joy and peace replaced the dread and sadness. It would be an emotional day. There was no doubt about that, but it would also be a blessing. That's how my son would have wanted it.

I made my way out of bed and the house was full and busy, everyone getting coffee, washing up, and getting ready. Kids yelled to find shoes and dress clothes or refused to get ready at all. I made my way to the coffee pot and poured myself the largest cup I could find. My aunt was sitting at the counter, her coffee in hand just looking at me. I reached across the counter, grabbed her hand and gave it a squeeze with a smile. I told her I was okay, knowing that is what she was wondering. I made my way back down the hall to shower and dress. As we each finished, making sure we all looked appropriate, I stepped out the door into the driveway. I would be riding with my cousin. The sun was bright and warm for September. It was beautiful and perfect, the way it danced through the tall maple trees, casting patterns of shadows all around. I tilted my head to feel the warmth on my face. I wanted to look at the clouds, to look at heaven, and to thank my son for such a beautiful day to remember him. As I did this, a butterfly floated down, interlacing between the cars. Once again, I knew my son was there. I knew my Kalen was with me. I tear dropped from my face, and I mouthed the words, "Thank you." I knew deep inside that my son created this beautiful day just for us. We gathered in the cars and made our way into town.

The church itself was beautiful, adorned with simple flowers and sprays. Arrangements honored Kalen's relationships. One said son, another brother, and still another said grandson. Down the center isle stood an alter adorned with flowers, and the urn that would soon contain Kalen's ashes. My dear friend, who spent the long summer days playing with me and the children, made the urn for us with her own hands. In the center of the urn hung a beautiful black and white photo of my boy. It captured his perfect smile, and the twinkle and glint in his eye. I dared not pass through the doors into that room, just yet. I merely looked and made my way to the fellowship hall.

I encountered an incredible scene there. So many beautiful people hurried about, preparing, organizing, and setting up for the lunch that would follow the service. It felt to me like a community of loving souls who came together to shine light into a dark corner of life. It felt less dim with them around. I felt grateful for every single one of them, then and still now. As I made my way into the main church to take my seat, the images before me carried intense gravity. There, in the center, was the alter adorned with the photo of my son and directly behind it, hung the cross. I felt instantly transported back to the little chapel in the hospital where I cursed God. Now, my beautiful God held me in his arms, despite my previous anger. This same God held my Kalen in his arms too – right there in front of me. Tears began to fall down my face as I accessed a sea of emotions. Each tear carried something out of me. In the salty water, I released my grief, heartache, anger, and despair to this image in front of me. With each tear, those holes inside me filled with gratitude. I had a lot to be grateful for. My Kalen was at peace in heaven, and I got to be his father. My boys, as I said many times before, were and are my greatest gifts.

My family followed right behind me and began to fill in the pews. The only person missing was my mother. She remained in the hospital, weak from chemo and susceptible to every germ and parasite in existence. Though the doctors seemed willing to let her leave for a day, we did not want to tax her nor put her in danger. We insisted she stay there. We did, however, decide to record the service so she could watch it later. She deserved that closure for herself when she was healthy enough to watch it. I listened as people filled into the small church and soft hymns played in the background. While my ears engaged the surroundings, I could not bring myself to take my eyes off the table where my son's photo sat.

The pastor stepped up to the podium and a hushed silence fell over the room. The service began. I cannot tell you what he said in that moment. Words seemed to have little meaning to me right then – like utterances of white noise. My son looked at me through his photo. I could feel every part of me falling into an abyss as rocks crashed from a cliff into the churning chaos of the waters below. I felt myself sinking and being lost from sight, carried out and away. I was disappearing. It happened again – the disconnect and the cold, ugly truth. My son would never hold my hand again. I would never hug him or hear him call out my name. He would never love, hurt, laugh, or cry again; never feel accomplishment or defeat. There would be no teachable moments or new memories. All I had left now were the old ones. What if forgot them? What if the memories ceased to exist in my mind the way Kalen ceased to exist in the world? What if I never found that part of myself again?

I felt myself spiraling, when a hand gently landed on my shoulder, pulling me back from the abyss and out of the open waters where I lost myself. The pastor's touch retrieved me. I slowly rose and made my way to the front, my words and feelings sprawled out on a piece of paper. I read the following words out loud:

"Thank you all for coming today. Thank you for your love and your support. Thank you for sharing with me, this moment. I have spent a lot of time trying to find the right words, the words that would do my son justice. But how, how are there ever right words? A father should never utter these words. A father should never lay his child to rest. My son. My son was the definition of pure love, of pure light, of pure joy. His soul represented all the wonderful magic and mystery only a child can possess. Kalen lived to make others smile. He lived to make others laugh. To know my son was to love my son. It is that simple. Kalen loved Rudolph, he loved his toys, but most of all he loved his brother. There is no greater love or bond than that which Kalen shared with his brother. Where one would go, the other would follow. Kalen was selfless, always just wanting to help. He wanted to be a cop when he grew up."

I paused, finally looking up. For the first time, I saw all of the people who filled the space. There were so many people there, for my son and for me. The tears just came. They poured out of me. There was no holding them back any longer. Through my sobs, I continued.

"Kalen wanted to be a cop. He wanted to protect people when he was big and strong. Sadly, I couldn't protect him. My son was all the very best of me, and now there remains a hole in me that aches for his smile, to hear him giggle as he was about to do something he knew he wasn't supposed to. But, this is a time of celebration, a time for laughter, and hope. Kalen loved peanut-butter and grape jelly sandwiches. He loved anything peanut-butter if I am being honest. He loved picking the raspberries from my garden, thinking I hadn't noticed, or didn't notice his fruit-stained hands and face. Yes, my son was all things beautiful in this world. He was, as he said, my best bud! Rest easy my sweet, sweet angel, until Dee Dee sees you again."

I walked to where his urn rested and I gave him one final kiss, then I made my way back to my seat, where I lost myself completely to the sorrow. The rest of the service was a blur. My brother spoke next, but by then, all of my senses stopped working. All I knew was pain. It felt like I was trapped in a living death, and I wasn't sure in that moment if I could ever come back from it. I wanted to die. I wanted my boy back, but none of this could ever happen. As much as I asked for death in moments, to not exist would be the easy, selfish way out for me. I looked back at the cross. I had my faith. I knew God had a plan, and that all of this happened for a reason, even if I didn't know what that reason was yet. I knew I had to have faith.

The service ended, and we exited the church, walking slowly as we closed the door on this chapter of my journey. However, closing a door and closure were two entirely different things. I would not delude myself, but I did feel there was something more to come. In the lobby, my family and I lined ourselves up next to the doors. I wanted to make sure, to the best of my ability, to thank every person who had given up their time to share in honoring my son. I shook hands and hugged so many people – many of whom were strangers to me. Their faces registered, but who they actually were felt like a mystery in that moment. Finally, after the last of the guests were greeted, I made my way to the fellowship hall. It was filled with food and lovely people laughing, sharing stories, and telling jokes. There were hugs, and well wishes, and to my pure joy, nearly everyone was enjoying a peanut-butter and grape jelly sandwich. What a beautiful way to honor Kalen! Old friendships rekindled and new friendships formed over his childhood favorite. Seeing them there, eating PB&J's together, seemed truly special. With that, I needed some air.

I left and stepped outside, into the crisp sun at the height of the day. I raised my face to it, feeling the warmth of its rays. I closed my eyes and saw the red translucence of the light against my closed eyelids. Life did go on, and so would I. I knew my son found peace and I would too someday. For now, I simply was. The days rushed past after that. Good moments interspersed with not so good ones. Through it all I had a sense of great anticipation. It was time to bring Karter home; time to start our new journey together. I wanted it to be a journey of healing and love.

TWENTY-SEVEN:
HOMECOMING

We hit the road a couple of days after the funeral to pick up Karter. I scanned the collection of supplies I packed for him. Coloring books and crayons. Check. Portable DVD player and movies. Check. Pillow and blanket. Check. Toys and extra clothes. Check. For once, the list elicited a feeling of fulfillment and a sense of excited anticipation, rather than the dread-filled lists which fueled my forward momentum before. From the moment that gun sent a bullet wailing through the trailer where Kalen slept soundly in his bed, I endured an ice storm of trauma. It pummeled the earth with absolute brutality. Those other lists acted as armor, shielding me from death by a thousand cuts. They served a purpose, and so did this one.

I clicked my seatbelt and looked over at my cousin and my dad's friend, who gladly jumped back out of their lives to make this trip with me. We had come full circle in such a short amount of time. It seemed as inconceivable as landing on the moon once was. Less than 48 hours prior, we celebrated Kalen's life. Now we embraced a celebration of a different sort, and it brought my psyche a much-needed reprieve. When the last of the people left the funeral reception and the tears and talking quieted to a hush in the hallways of the church, people returned to their daily lives. I, on the other hand, became trapped in a slog, muddied and broken. Life stood still in the space between our elegies and this key turn in the ignition.

For most people the funeral marked an ending. For me, it triggered nightmares. When I laid down in bed and closed my eyes, the precious veil of sleep lit up like a runway at night. The gentle takeoff into restful solace transformed into a visual invasion of flashbacks. Behind my eyes, the images relentlessly pounded the airspace. I saw flashes of Kalen's body lying in the hospital bed and the bullet wound, which I had dressed and wrapped in a moment of tenderness and care. The scenes – so vivid and real – jolted me awake, drenched in sweat as tears streamed down my cheeks. At the time, I kept it to myself and forced a smile on my face, thinking if I just acted normal, things might be normal. I tried to will my way into coping.

Now, with the humming of the highway, I set my sights on Karter. I dialed the number of the foster home in South Carolina and listened to the trill of the line. "We're on the way," I reported to my son. I could feel his energetic excitement from 660 miles away. My phone call with the social worker did not contain that same excitement. It seemed bluntly obvious to me, neither she, not her supervisor, nor the courts appreciated this turn of events. They vehemently disagreed with the ruling in New York and did not want Karter removed from South Carolina. "Why?" I wondered warily. Had not this "system" – this series of public agencies – failed already? Had they not dropped the ball when neighbors noticed the situation with my kids or when probation failed to enact repercussions when my ex-wife's boyfriend acted out of line? Had they not allowed a woman who lived with a known felon, banned from owning a firearm, to purchase a gun herself and place it in the home? What made these pompous authorities believe they had a better chance of protecting Karter and that I was too risky to bet on. Alas, it no longer mattered. They had to comply and frankly, at that point, I could care less what they thought.

As the minutes ticked by, we passed fields and forests, waterways and cities, railroads, and thousands of people headed to their own destinations. The license plates changed, and the landscapes transformed, as we chunked away at the miles and closed the space between me and my sons. I wasn't just picking up Karter on this trip. The phone rang along the way and when I answered, I heard the voice of the funeral director. "Kalen's ashes are ready," he reported, "and you can pick them up when you are in town." So many times, through my addiction and my sobriety, I dreamed of the moment I would have my boys. I never wanted it this way, but things happened and now I had no choice but to bring one boy home to a life I knew I could provide, while the other came home in a small black box.

We began to close in on our destination and with it, a swirling tornado of emotions unexpectedly swept me up into its chaotic funnel. My excitement remained, but just as tree limbs and rocks and pieces of houses bang against one another in the circling wind, other feelings broke off inside me. We neared the eye of the storm

– the place which personified my deepest fears and pain. With each mile we got closer to Hartsville, a pervasive sadness swirled around jolts of anxiety. Dread set in. I told myself, "This is irrational. A place does not have to contain the fiber of what occurred there." Yet, I hated it. I truly hated this place. I let go of the internal struggle and accepted that Hartsville may always be a mirror for me, of what occurred there.

At long last, we arrived at the very same building where, only a week before, I threatened the director of the department as he sat behind his big wooden desk. This was the place I said goodbye to my boy twice, promising to return; the place where I told him his brother died. In the parking lot, I felt a sense of amazement that this turn of events occurred so quickly. I climbed out of the truck and made my way to the front doors of the building. The worker stood waiting for me. She told me Karter was in route, as well as his mother. During the drive, I spoke on the phone with my ex-wife and let her know that Kalen's ashes could be picked up. She asked if she and her parents could meet me at the Department of Social Services. They wanted to bring Karter's belongings for us to take back to New York. They read off a list, like an inventory: clothes, toys, his bedding, extra blankets, a bicycle, and finally, his pet snake. I recoiled at the idea of having a snake in the truck, but I would do anything to make Karter feel safe and welcome. He lost too much already. I wasn't about to let him lose anymore.

The worker confirmed receipt of the court order and the warrant from the judge in New York, indicating a green light on our pickup. I signed a batch of documents and strolled back outside to wait for my son. The first vehicle which arrived in the lot carried my ex-wife and her parents. I felt a little shocked to see her father still there, knowing he rarely liked to travel. They piled out, as I made my way to greet them. Right away, I noticed the truck bed, filled with garbage bags containing what I assumed to be Karter's belongings. I saw a few boxes, the bicycle, and inside the truck, his snake enclosure. We made small talk as we transferred the items from their truck to ours. Just as we finished the transfer, a van pulled up kitty corner from us, and out jumped Karter.

His smile looked bigger than ever, beaming, and full of joy and excitement. The sun caught his eyes just so, and they sparkled brilliantly. In that moment, I felt like I was seeing him for the very first time. My heart tore open and the love just spilled out. He ran across the parking lot and into my arms. "Dee Dee, you came back. You promised. You came back," he shouted as he jumped into me. I hugged him as tight as I could. This time I would never have to let him go – not ever. He was my son, and nothing in the world could keep us apart ever again.

After he spent some time hugging, kissing, and talking with his mother and grandparents, the moment came to close this chapter and begin the long drive home. They promised to see Karter soon and I assured them, they could call anytime and see him as often as they wanted to. We briefly discussed my ex-wife's upcoming court appearance in New York, though I had little to offer. Regarding her situation, I simply had no clue what the future held. The most important thing now was that I busted Karter out of foster care and, finally, he could come home.

In the truck, Karter and I crawled into the big back seat. I wanted to be as close to him as possible, but before we could mark zero on the odometer, commemorating the start of our homecoming, we had one more stop to make. I entered the funeral home feeling uncertain. This piece of the puzzle felt weighty, and it settled on my shoulders as I walked inside. The funeral director who peppered me with questions and took my check the last time I came, met me inside the front doors. He walked me back to the very same room where I made the call to cremate my son. On the table sat a black, rectangular, plastic box. Inside, lay Kalen's remains, filtered down to ash. I signed a piece of paper on which I verified receipt of the ashes, and he handed me the box. I looked down at it, sitting inside my palms, my fingers wrapped around its sharp edges. This was all that was left of Kalen. His entire five years on earth fit inside a small, nine inch by six inch, plastic box. I began to cry gently and as I wept, I thanked the man. As strange as it sounds, I felt incredibly comforted. I had him. Both my boys were coming home.

With the thump-thump of the long and winding highway, Karter and I colored and watched movies. We talked about the woods around my cousin's house and all the exploring we would do. Karter listed off a litany of all his favorite things and I consumed every word like vital nutrition for my soul. He educated me for some time on the proper care of snakes and all I could think of was, "Together at last." This wasn't just a union I desperately sought during the tragedy of the past two weeks. Every cell and drop of blood in my body hummed with intent for years, trying to get back to my boys. Now the sound of his perfect little voice in this little cave we created in the backseat replaced the internal ringing of desperation I long battled against. "Together at last."

As the road lengthened and stretched in front of us, sleepiness crept across Karter's face. He needed rest too. Just like when he was a baby, he reached out to hold my hand as he fell asleep. With every breath, in and out, I grasped his little hand. I knew, then and there, that whatever life brought our way, it was him and me, together forever. I watched him sleeping until I too fell asleep. For the very first time since all of this started, I slept in peace. A vast comfort filled the cracks and corners of my being and I truly rested, my heart settled at last.

Twenty-Eight:
A Gun, a Trial, a Confession

WHILE I STAYED SOBER after Kalen passed away, I struggled intensely with my pain. It took a long while to see the gifts that came out of my suffering. I see them now. God gave me a chance to fulfill my purpose as a father. I got to be there for my son, and I held him. I took care of him in that critical moment. For a long time through my life, I struggled with doubts. I often wondered, was I a terrible father? By honoring Kalen's life, I learned that I did many things right and I needed to let go of the guilt. Others had to face their own consequences, guilt, and society's judgement.

The solicitor general personally handled Kalen's case, while I worked together with a victim advocate. I later had been told, whether true or not, that the area Kalen was killed had the highest child death-by-gun rate in the entire United States. Yet, somehow, this felt different. Kalen's death shook that state and community to the core. It was all everyone talked about. The story headlined every newspaper and all the major news outlets throughout the trial. When people realized who I was, they would often come up to me sobbing. I didn't know these people; they were complete strangers. Part of why I think the community suffered so much revolved around the fact that my ex-wife served as a trusted and loved fifth and sixth grade math teacher.

Neighbors messaged me saying, "I wish I would have done something sooner." People told me my kids were always at their house eating or bathing. I heard people throw around the words fighting and domestic violence. They told me there were times my ex-wife passed out or that the kids were locked out of the house while temperatures reached over 100 degrees outside. They recounted horror stories of my kids drinking out of a mud puddle. So many departments dropped the ball. Probation had been to the house and saw my kids. They were aware my ex-wife's boyfriend violated probation three times but never cited him. I wondered, would my son still be alive if someone had done something? If someone had just reached out and told me what was happening, would Kalen not have died? Rage and resentment filled me to the brim, but I never lashed out. I never hurt anyone. Sometimes, I still revel in the fact that I did not lose my mind.

From day one, my ex-wife's boyfriend pled guilty. He never tried to hide what he did. In fact, he didn't even request an attorney. They found him and he said, "I did it." It was that simple. What we learned throughout the trail and testimonies painted a fuller picture of the hours before and after the shooting. It was a Friday night after a full week of school and both boys had soccer games that evening. As parents do, they decided to divide and conquer. He took Kalen and she took Karter. After their games, they all met back home and ate dinner. He gave the boys a bath and sat down

T.R. Sherlock

with Kalen to read him a book. The boys always shared a bed even though they had their own rooms. In an unusual move, Kalen told Karter he wanted to sleep in his own bed that night. He said he wanted to be a big boy.

My ex-wife and her boyfriend apparently regularly drank and took drugs. She was extremely intoxicated. They fought and she passed out. During court and sentencing, her boyfriend recalled his final moments with Kalen. They finished reading a story and Kalen looked up at him and said, "I love you. You are my best friend!" Then Kalen asked if he could call him daddy. He told Kalen you already have a daddy. Kalen announced, "I already talked to Dee Dee, and he said it was okay." Kalen had talked to me about it that summer and I knew how much he loved this man. I had no problem with it. So, he told Kalen he could call him daddy too.

After the boys were safely tucked into bed, he went back out into the living area and continued drinking. He began cleaning his gun, which he normally kept under the kitchen sink. He said he didn't know the gun was loaded and as he went to put it away, it accidentally went off. The bullet traveled through the wall and struck Kalen in the head, in his bedroom. Frankly, none of it seemed plausible to me. After the gun went off, my ex-wife apparently woke up. Karter awoke as well to the sound of mommy screaming, "What happened?" Karter recounted, "She ran by me and was dripping all this red stuff." He wandered to Kalen's room and saw more of the red stuff, like someone took a balloon and splattered it on the wall.

She grabbed Kalen and took off in the car. When her boyfriend realized she left and saw Karter standing there, he exclaimed, "Your mom left you here, oh my god!" He put Karter on the coach, covered him in a blanket, gave him a popsicle, and turned on some cartoons. Then, he cleaned the gun, walked out into a field, and buried it in a Teenage Mutant Ninja Turtle lunch box. Meanwhile, my ex-wife drove to the Carolina Pines Regional Medical Center Emergency Room. The nurse's and police reports said she entered the hospital calmly as if nothing happened. She said, excuse me, my son has been shot and he needs to see a doctor. She asked if someone could grab her purse and move her car that was parked out front. The hospital called 911.

The police showed up at their residence with search dogs because her boyfriend wasn't there. He was hiding in a field adjacent to the property. It wasn't long before they found the gun and found Karter alone in the house watching cartoons. When they found her boyfriend, they never even had to ask a question. He looked up and said, "I shot him." Out of all the men my ex-wife had been with, I loved this one. Kalen adored him. During that last summer visit to New York, I remember Kalen saying to me, "Dee Dee, you know you are my best friend, right?" I said, of course I do. Kalen asked, "Is it okay if I have two best friends?" I told him yes. He said his mom's boyfriend was his other best friend. He said he loved him, and he was "the coolest." That was when Kalen asked me if he could call his mommy's boyfriend daddy. I felt happy for him, to have joy in his life like that. I answered, "Absolutely buddy!"

I found out later when everything was revealed and there were no more secrets, that man taught the boys how to bathe properly because their mom had not been bathing them. He would wake them up at 11:00 p.m. or midnight after she passed out and take them swimming with glow lights, the remnants of which I saw when I sat at their trailer that day. He wanted to give them the fun they needed at that time in their lives. Later, he shared that the only reason he stayed was to protect the kids. He was absolutely destroyed that he killed the little boy who loved him more than anything in the world.

Twenty-Nine:
Forgiveness

At sentencing, the court afforded me the opportunity to present a victim's impact statement to the judge. I wrote pages, in preparation. I made the 12-hour drive to the courthouse in South Carolina that day with my sponsor, full of vengeance. I went there for one reason: to get justice for my son. Such a big word: justice. The word I once scoffed at in the investigator's office in South Carolina now consumed me. Turns out, those seven letters did not mean what I thought they meant. I wanted the shooter to pay; to get the punishment I felt he deserved for killing my son. I heard the words he spoke during the trial. I knew what happened and I understood his story, but I felt hatred and rage. Forgiving him remained the furthest thing from my mind.

Then he walked into the courtroom. It had been nine months

since Kalen's death, and this was the last entrance he would make before the judge decided his punishment. As he made his way to his seat, I saw something in him I had not seen before. He looked like a broken man. I recognized his pain immediately. I'm a recovered addict; I know what brokenness looks like, and I suddenly saw the truth of what happened. When it became my turn to speak, I walked up to the podium. A woman who worked with me on the victim's impact statement and the district attorney stood beside me. I held up a picture of Kalen in my hands, lifting it for the judge to see. What came next surprised even me. I did not read what I had written. Instead, I spoke from the heart. As best as I can remember, this is what I shared:

"Your honor, this is my son. This little boy will never laugh again. This little boy will never lose a tooth. This little boy just learned to ride his bike without training wheels. He will never win a soccer game. Never fall in love. Never have his heart broken. Because that man took it."

"I could have been that man. Every time I got behind the wheel, drunk or stoned, I could have taken someone's life. Every time I gave a drug to someone, I could have killed them. By the grace of God, I did not. I will never understand what it is to take a human life, and I cannot do that now. That little boy loved this man and trusted him. My son was all about love for people; about compassion and doing the right thing even when we don't want to."

I turned and looked at the defendant and said:

"I forgive you. I can't be mad at you because I could have been you, but understand, the opportunity you are being given is a gift. I don't want to hear that you are suicidal. You don't get to die. Your punishment is to live and to live with this. Your life is not your own anymore. Your life is my son's. You have to make something good out of this. You owe it to him. A little boy was your best friend, and you took that from yourself and from me; but I will not take someone else's son away. If I do, I am no better. Your honor, I ask that you allow the plea deal that was offered."

The judge looked at me, astonished. "Are you serious?" he asked. I said that I was. I looked at the man again and I said, "Damn it, you owe my son. You do not get to die. You do not get to escape the consequences of this." There wasn't a dry eye in the room. The judge, still dumbfounded, said in all his years, he never saw anything like that. He turned to the defendant and said, "[Sir], I hope you understand the immense gift you've just been given."

A moment – a split second – is all it took for my son to die, and it was all it took for me to find forgiveness. It was a split second when my heart decided someone else's son should live – really live. I remember saying to the judge, "This must stop. No more hurt. No more loss. Somewhere along the line the chain of events must be done." I just could not take this human being away from his mom and his family; to deprive them of laughter and family dinners; to put him behind a plate of glass where they could not touch him or hug him. There was no chance of Kalen ever coming back and I did not want this man's family to suffer that loss with him. The choice had a clear domino effect.

Today, the man who shot my son is a wonderful person. Sadly, he'll never escape the past, but he is clean and sober. He works and he speaks to at-risk youth about the dangers of living like he did. He shares Kalen's story. My act of forgiveness allowed that man to continue Kalen's work in this life – to make a positive change and help others learn compassion. That was my son. He really did, in many ways, have a greater purpose in his death than even in his life. I know those are two diametrically opposed ideas – that there can be value in death. I have come to believe it anyway because my God had a purpose. The universe had a purpose for all of this, and I had to get out of my own way and my own grief to see it.

PROLOGUE:
MAKING SENSE OF IT ALL

I<small>N</small> <small>THE</small> <small>TIME</small> <small>JUST</small> after Kalen's death, I faced immeasurable guilt. I felt like everything good inside of me went into my kids. When they left – for a weekend or to move to South Carolina – nothing good remained; I felt awful inside. My drug and alcohol abuse ensued, and I could not be there for them. When I finally got sober and got back to them, I sensed an urgency to do everything I had not been doing – not just for me but for all of us.

I did not get to do all those things. Rather, I suddenly found myself being asked to do the hardest thing of all. As Kalen lay in the hospital room in a coma, I had to kiss his boo-boo; a boo-boo that could never be fixed. I also had another child to care for. I had to tell him his brother died; to face real monsters, not the imaginary ones under the bed; to teach forgiveness; to reestablish a relationship with their mother; and to battle the thousands of questions in my own mind.

I learned to look long and hard at how I was feeling in any given moment; to make sure I never placed my reactions or judgements onto my son. I came to understand that, today, I am part of a fraternity of parents of lost children. The initiation fee – the dues you pay to enter this fraternity - is the loss of your child. You are initiated through an inferno, a baptismal fire. No one wants to be a part of this group, yet here I am. I have walked the flame and burned in the heat, and I have risen above it in honor of my sons – one living, one dead.

I say we glow brighter. We are survivors of the greatest pain that exists in the world – one there is no word for. Other losses have a definable name. You are a victim, an orphan, or a widow. There is no word in the English language that describes a parent who has suffered the death of a child. When people find out about it, they shy away. They often stop looking you in the eye. You become broken or damaged to them; they see the experience as foreign and unnatural. Some people say nothing and avoid you altogether. That is what this fraternity brings you – unanswered questions, undefinable concepts, silence, awkward encounters, intense pain, and the prospect of your own guilt.

Down this long and arduous road, I overcame so many obstacles. After all this time I have come to believe that, too often, people take for granted what it means to be a parent - the awesome responsibility and gift of it all. We do not own our children. God created the essence of their being in his vision. It is more than genetics and science. A part of your essence goes in them as well. I like to think that my sons got the best of all of us. If you are not willing to give everything of who you are as a parent, you may not deserve the gift. I know I did not do everything right all the time, but I did give it everything I had. I was and I am dad, protector, and nurturer. I had to take care of my son no matter the cost; he came first. I learned this through my own recovery.

Every day, I make sure to bask in the glory and wonderfulness of my children. The God of my understanding, the creator of life, put them in my hands and I try not to take them for granted for a single moment. I know that as soon as I say, look at what I did, I can lose it. When I put more value in the things around me, I can lose it all.

What is left at the end of the day? When I look at my own life and I think about Kalen, or I watch Karter as he grows, I have a simple mantra. Taking on the example of my creator, I think, "My child, this is for you. Know that I carry the yoke you carry. Your burden is my burden. Your hardship is my hardship. When you cry, I cry. This is my gift to you." My life is a song for Kalen.

Epilogue: Afterwards

THERE ARE SO MANY stories and so many facts I could add to this book from before, during, and after losing my son. Suffice it to say, what you have read captures the essence of my experience. Still, as a reader, you may have questions.

The man convicted of killing Kalen received a 15-year suspended sentence after my offer of a plea deal. He had five years to serve and was released in two on parole. Part of the conditions of his release included treatment for recovery and speaking. From what I can gather from the parole board and some limited conversations I have had with his mother, he remains sober and healthy today. He lives at home and works, while in his free time, he speaks at prisons and to at-risk youth about the dangers of drugs and guns. I have a lifetime restraining order in place against him and do not communicate with him directly. Some details of what happened that evening came up after the trial. Hearing those details, I began to wonder if I had the entire story. However, those details will never see the light of day, nor can this case ever be retried in court. Still, I often wonder what the fuller story is.

My ex-wife also faced charges for her role the night that Kalen died. Those charges included allowing infliction of great bodily injury upon a child and two counts of unlawful neglect of a child. She had prior knowledge of her boyfriend's previous conviction and that he was not allowed to own a firearm. She signed paperwork for him to live with her. She then bought the guns and registered them in her name.

When the prosecutor called me in preparation for court, I knew exactly what I wanted. I wanted her in prison. Then, one beautiful afternoon back in New York, Karter and I walked through woods visiting with his grandparents. "Can I see mommy," he asked. Then, he continued, "Should I not like mommy?" The questions swirled through my mind, challenging me to dig a little deeper. Later that night as I lay in bed helping him fall asleep, Karter asked, "Do you think mommy is a bad person?" I looked at him thoughtfully and responded with my own question. "Why do you ask that?" A change began to take place inside of me.

Karter would decide for himself over time what he thought of the events from his childhood, and the type of relationship he wanted with the woman who brought him into this world. I did not want to insert my own biases into that, but I did need to protect him. Ultimately, I agreed to another plea deal. Some people criticize me for that move, but over these years since Kalen died, it has proven to be the best way for Karter to process his experiences and move forward. I do not apologize for my decisions.

In August 2018, she pled guilty to that plea deal which included a common law misdemeanor for breach of peace, aggravated in nature. She also lost her teaching license and was placed on the child abuse registry. To this day, visitations with her son remain supervised.

Karter has evolved into a wonderful and beautiful boy. In school, he is number one in his class. He has a passion and love for animals and hopes to become a veterinarian. He plays soccer and runs track, hunts and fishes, and is your all-American boy. I went on to advocate and serve as a resource for fathers in the family court system. I co-founded On Demand Mediation, LLC and E-Court Coach Consulting LLC. I have also served as an office manager and aid in the legal industry. With bachelor's degrees in English Language Literature and Clinical Psychology, and a master's in Clinical Psychology, I served for a time as a licensed substance abuse and mental health counselor in the state of New York. But the most important accomplishment of my life will forever remain being a father. Watching my son Karter grow has been the greatest blessing of my life.

As *A Song for Kalen* comes into existence and the words on the pages reach out to touch lives around the world, I want my readers to use this story to gain a greater understanding of our shared humanity. I garnered that fuller understanding being a father who traversed the road from birth to death with Kalen and Karter. Before the events in this book occurred, I had a socially constructed understanding of what it meant to be human. Facing such a tragedy challenged me at my deepest level and forced to me live that humanity. It forced me to transcend my own pain to find a space inside myself where life could flourish – a space of forgiveness, love, and compassion. In each moment and each decision – each flash of rage and each eruption of despair – I had to transcend. It became the only real way to generate a healthy environment for me and my son.

At its most basic level, this book is about finding my humanity, where seemingly, little humanity existed. I had to find something apart from myself in order to generate life in the wake of my son's passing. I had to learn to say goodbye. I had to tell Karter his brother died. I had to learn how to be angry but still function. I had to learn the difference between vengeance and justice, to step outside myself time and time again, against the worst of odds. My behavior, though not always perfect, would serve as an example to my son. When he asked me that quiet evening, as we lay in bed, "Is my mom a bad person," I could have manipulated the situation to justify my emotions. I did not. I learned humanity, once again. I navigated so many moving pieces without causing more pain, and I did not do it as a martyr. I did not boast about the cross I bore, saying, "Look how great I am!" I am flawed like anyone else. Yet, here, in Kalen's song, we find a truth so perfect, it reveals the potential for good inside each one of us. I hope you find it too, and in doing so, give meaning to Kalen's life.

Further Reading:

- Woman charged after allowing felon boyfriend to have gun that killed her son, deputies say (wyff4.com)

- Father offers forgiveness to 5-year-old son's killer - Orato World Media

- Warrants allege Hartsville man charged in boy's shooting death was impaired while handling loaded gun (wmbfnews.com)

- Man sentenced in shooting death of 5-year-old Hartsville boy (wbtw.com)

- Local family tries to find healing after South Carolina gun death of 5-year-old | News | oleantimesherald.com

- Hartsville man pleads guilty to manslaughter for shooting death of 5-year-old boy (wmbfnews.com)

- Olean father forgives South Carolina man who accidentally shot his son, hopes for reform | News | oleantimesherald.com

- Olean man asks Judge to forgive the man who shot and killed his son (wivb.com)

Made in United States
North Haven, CT
28 June 2023

38358226R00114